Table For Three?

Bringing Your Smart Phone To Lunch & 50 Dumb Mistakes Smart Managers <u>Don't</u> Make!

Darryl Rosen

ISBN: 0615575544
ISBN-13: 978-0615575544

To Jill, Josh, Danny and Ben.

Welcome to the start of what I'm sure will be a successful journey eliminating the mistakes that smart managers <u>don't</u> make.

Is this book for you? I think so.

Do you manage employees, associates, sales professionals or anyone else on a regular basis? Do you rely on others to pay your bills – to put food on the table?

And now the tough question:

Do you make the occasional mistake as you navigate the treacherous waters of management?

Then this book is for you!

I am delighted to share my lessons from running a successful business and my recent interactions with so many intelligent, thought-provoking, hard working management professionals.

My thoughts are based, in part, on literally hundreds of coaching sessions with management professionals all over the country. In these pages, I've tried to share a sense of how managers operate and I've identified 50 avoidable mistakes that smart managers <u>don't</u> make.

Your efforts, should you take this endeavor seriously, will leave you *better than before*. Better able to handle what a manager handles on a daily basis.

You'll be more professional, confident and proactive and you may even develop an associate or professional along the way. All good things in my book.

So, if you have the courage to start the process, then you will be well on your way towards achieving stronger management practices and the results will follow. You will be more successful. Why? Because…

…That's just the way it works.

Thank you!
Darryl Rosen

P.S. For more information and tools to help you make great use of this book, please visit – www.tableforthreethebook.com

CONTENTS

INTRODUCTION

Do you mind if I ask you a question?

Are you thinking, "What up with the cover of this book?"

That's a fair question. I'll explain, but first, let me tell you a story.

Many years ago I was the President and Owner of a business in Chicago called Sam's Wines & Spirits. We employed over 200 hardworking beverage professionals. One beautiful summer day, a wine buyer of ours asked me to have lunch. By the tone of his invitation, I sensed that he had something on his mind.

We had lunch.

But I should have left my Blackberry in my office.

My wife, the lovely Jill, called a few minutes into the meal. I ignored the call. Before you ask, this was after the advent of cell phones, but before the phenomenon of texting took over our lives.

Yes, younger readers, there was life before texting!

Anyway, she called back a few minutes later. I ignored the call again, but now I was wondering what she wanted. You know how that goes. After the second call, you start to get concerned. While at first I was giving Bill my full attention, I slowly began shifting my thoughts away from him.

His body seemed to sag a bit.

Then she called again.

Is the house on fire? I pondered. I answered the call.

We exchanged pleasantries.

"Honey, I'll be back at my desk in a few minutes," I explained.

"I just have one question," she responded.

"It will just be a few minutes. I'll call you!" I countered, although she probably knew I'd forget.

(This isn't her first rodeo. She knows ADD when she sees it…)

Anyway, she paused. It was a really long pause. So long I thought the call had dropped.

Nope. She was still there. She wasn't going to be denied.

1

"Do you want grilled zucchini with your dinner?" she blurted out.

Really? That's why you needed to reach me so desperately? (Notice: there aren't any quotes around the preceding sentence. I wouldn't say that to her. I like sleeping in the bedroom!)

Anyway, you should have seen the look on Bill's face. You know how it's common these days to say, "Really?" when someone does something stupid or unexpected?

Yes, a picture can say a thousand words, and Bill's expression said just that – long before it was such a common expression in our culture. His look said what his mouth didn't need to say.

Really?

I answered Jill because, after all, it was a simple question and she wasn't giving up. "Um…yes."

Who doesn't love grilled zucchini in the middle of the summer? Unless the rules have changed, I think it's still a vegetable and it's mighty tasty.

Anyway, Bill made some excuse about having to check in a White Burgundy order and our lunch ended rather abruptly. I never learned what was on his mind. He left the company just a few months after our lunch. I learned later that there was no White Burgundy order that day.

I committed a big mistake that day; a mistake that smart managers don't make. It should have been just Bill and I, but through my actions, I invited a third.

Table for three?

Let's go back to the cover for a moment.

What is the manager in the illustration talking about? Who knows?

Maybe he's talking to his wife or girlfriend, or possibly his mistress. Maybe he's instructing his bookie to lay a few dollars down on the Cubs game (sadly, I'd go with the opponent – it doesn't really matter who they're playing). Maybe it's a long lost friend from his favorite college course – Underwater Basket Weaving!

It doesn't really matter because he isn't *dancing with the one that brung him*, as the expression goes.

I certainly wasn't dancing with Bill that day, literally or figuratively. I have two left feet and hardly an ear for rhythm. I'm usually the one clapping - when nobody else is clapping…

But I digress. Let's be serious for a moment.

In Table for Three?, Using Your Smart Phone at Lunch & 50 Other Mistakes Smart Managers Don't Make, I share my experiences in managing, leading and coaching hundreds of managers. I'll draw upon numerous conversations and share solutions to many common and not-so-common mistakes. I'll put many thoughts in your head. I'll ask you a ton of questions. I'll speak the plain and simple truth and, by the end, you'll have a few areas of your game to work on.

Through these pages, I'll also introduce you to 1) my family (Jill, Josh, Danny and Ben) and 2) my un-dying, sad, pathetic love for the Chicago Cubs. That's the Chicago baseball team that hasn't won a World Series in over 100 years – if you can't tell Chicago's teams apart. If you fancy the other team – there are exits on both sides of this aircraft, if you know what I mean.

Just kidding, you can read on as well.

Let's go back to the subject du jour.

I like to say that it's simple, but not easy. It's simple to want to avoid making the mistakes that great managers don't make, but not easy to avoid much of what I'll identify over the following pages.

I feel empathy for today's manager, who has to do so much more with fewer resources than even just a few years ago. It can't be easy, but I'm here to help.

One quick note: As you'll remember if you've read my other books, I end every chapter with the expression, "That's just the way it works!"

Why?

Well, I used this phrase in a presentation some time ago and it really resonated with the audience. Now I use it all the time. In my view, this phrase implies that there are certain principles that have force in manager/employee interaction no matter the situation.

For example, if you insult your sales professional's intelligence, he or she will rightly take offense. Your relationship will suffer – and that's just the way it works. There really isn't any further explanation needed.

Thanks for making it this far in my latest book. When my books sell, my boys are fond of saying, "Dad, another goofball bought one of your books."

They also say that listening to me give a presentation makes a good punishment for prisoners.

But that's a story for another day.

The great news is that I don't see you as a goofball and I have no doubt you'll use some of the strategies within. Should you do so, you will improve communication and increase the respect with which you treat your people. If you have expertise to share (and I'm sure you do!), your people will listen more. Increased respect equals increased acceptance of your coaching and development efforts. Better results will be just around the corner.

It's not easy, but I know you'll get there.

That's just the way it works!

MISTAKE 1

ACTING LIKE A WEENIE

I wanted a stronger title for this chapter. As I brainstormed, I came up with a lot of, shall we say, more descriptive terms for what we can reasonably call managers who say or do what we'll discuss in this chapter. In the end, it was a duel between acting like a weenie and acting like a bonehead. The weenie won. It's much classier.

Do you act like a weenie? Do you ever make mistakes that could categorize you as such? Sure, we all make mistakes, but some mistakes are more about processes. Not being clear enough, not sharing the basics of business, being too complacent, and so on – those mistakes are more easily corrected. Others mistakes come from, well, acting like a weenie or not caring about others. Take your pick. They're the same.

In this chapter we'll cover the type of judgment lapses that make one a weenie. Bad judgment. Poor judgment. Misguided judgment. Doing the wrong thing judgment. Any lapse in judgment where the needs, interests, goals and in some cases the welfare of employees and associates are ignored.

Thankfully, many of the mistakes in Table for Three? Can be reversed by learning a few skills. I wish that were the case with judgment mistakes, but these errors typically have a profound and disastrous impact on relationships.

For example, mistakes like communicating unclearly, (see mistake 8) lead to poor results, but the words and actions below lead to a far darker place. Like to an off-track betting parlor in the following story:

A sales professional at one of my distributors was called in by his team leader to deliver some POS to a customer, despite the fact that he (the sales professional) was on vacation. It wasn't a popular move around the office, and even less popular when the team leader's car was spotted parked outside an off-track betting parlor – for several hours. I hope he won big that day because, clearly, the team leader had more important things to do than to help his guy out. He broke a bond of trust, choosing to play the thoroughbreds instead of taking care of his own thoroughbreds. Hopefully, he took Secretariat in the 7th. Seemed like a shoe-in to me.

Was this guy a weenie or what?

And there are other examples as well. Over the years, I've asked many professionals to share their managers' ridiculous comments and actions with me.

Here are a few of the good ones (and by good, I mean terrible):

- "Telling me my sales suck!"
- "Telling me that management is going to do it their way, no matter what feedback they get."
- "Placing undue and overblown emphasis on short-term sales goals that don't assist me in creating better relationships with customers."
- "Getting upset with me over something I can't control."
- "Not taking my opinion into consideration."
- "Telling me they don't pay me to think!" (Note: life is too short to work for someone who would say that.)
- "Giving me the pleasure of a 60-minute rant at the end of the day, during my family time, dictating how I should have handled an execution issue that wasn't clearly explained to me in the first place."
- "Being told that I didn't get a job I had already been doing."
- "Telling me I'm not getting a raise promised to me by management."
- "Posting a new position and telling me that I shouldn't have applied, even though I was interested and qualified."
- "Not giving me important information in a timely manner."
- "Dragging his heels on my vacation request until after the cheap fares were gone!"
- "Showing impatience when I don't understand directions."
- "Waiting until the last minute to tell me what's going on."
- "Focusing on one negative instead of all the positives."
- "Throwing me under the bus."
- "Telling me nobody game me permission to do what I did to save the customer relationship."
- "Micromanaging me on every aspect of my job."
- "Calling me out in front of a customer."
- "Telling me he will take it under advisement."

That last bullet comes with a follow-up question. What does taking it under advisement really mean anyway? Well, according to an article I read online in Bloomberg Business Week, it may be your manager suggesting, "I'm not going to do whatever you just suggested I do, and I want you to know that I value your opinion less than I can tell you!" Wow, that's productive!

A good litmus test might be – if you wouldn't say that to your spouse, don't say it to your professionals. There are just certain words we don't use in real life! (Your current wife, not the one you discarded!)

By the way, telling someone you'll think about it, when you have no intention of thinking about it, is a real weenie move.

And there are more. My personal favorite was the professional who nominated his supervisor as the leader of the weenies. More often than not, the supervisor would answer the phone by saying, *"I'm busy. Make it fast."*

That wasn't after the hello – that was the hello.

He was a real weenie.

Many errors in judgment boil down to respect and consideration. Ask yourself the following questions:

Do you respect that your people have jobs to do? Are you being as considerate as possible? Are you weighing how your actions might affect your professionals? Do you believe that treating people well leads to success, or do you think that people have to do well before you treat them nicely?

In the example above, *Mr. Weenie* clearly didn't realize how his actions made him the poster child for the weenie movement. His associate, Mark, was afraid to call and to ask questions. When he did muster up the courage, *Mr. Weenie*, as you would imagine, wasn't so keen on hearing Mark out. He wasn't the best listener. Usually, after a few seconds of narrative, he would jump in with some half-grilled advice or a bad solution. Mark was never very keen on implementing *Mr. Weenie's* ideas. The thought of it made him boil…

Mr. Weenie didn't care that Mark was much closer to the situation than he was. And Mark resented that immensely. He hated that Mr. Weenie would jump in to try and save the day when, often, all Mark wanted was a sounding board.

Not to mention that *Mr. Weenie* usually had an answer for everything. He took credit for the good ones and threw Mark under the bus for the bad ones. That's not kosher in my book. (Sorry about all the hot dog references. I can't help myself…)

They say that employees quit their managers long before they quit their company. Unfortunately, I lost track of Mark after he gave his notice. Wherever he is, I hope he found someone who gives him a bit more time to get his ideas out. My hope is that his new manager weighs how his actions affect his people. I hope he's not acting like a weenie.

So, don't make what is perhaps the worst mistake that smart managers don't make. You'll have a more cohesive and engaged team, and good people like Mark won't seek greener pastures elsewhere. (Plus, weenies usually get cooked, and you don't want that! That grill can get awfully hot.)

That's just the way it works.

MISTAKE 2

ALLOWING MERCHANDISING SHORTCUTS

On a recent visit to Ohio, I took a team of sales professionals on a field trip to a retail store. The store we visited had a great selection and attentive, personalized service.

It was the kind of shop I'd welcome in my community.

As with most retail stores, though, I noticed plenty of opportunities to improve merchandising and signage.

The most striking example was a multiple-case display of Tito's Handmade Vodka just inside the store. Talk about premium real estate! The Tito's was right on the beach, if you know what I mean. It was situated in a real focal point for consumers entering the store, and it wasn't located too close to the entrance, which isn't the best place to be.

Strangely, there was just one small sign on the front of the display with the product's name and price. It wasn't easily identifiable and did nothing to improve the display or promote the vodka in a productive manner. The sign didn't engage, nor did it inform.

My first thought was "What about the story?" Come on! Tito's Handmade Vodka! The story practically writes itself.

It got me thinking…

What are the benefits of "handmade" vodka? Does that style of production affect the taste? Does it affect the mix-ability? What about glutens? Many people can't have glutens. Tito's is gluten-free. That's pretty cool. What about the company that produces Tito's? An entrepreneur makes this vodka in the heart of Texas. Yes, it's made in the good ol' USA! Most of those facts (and many others that can be learned just by clicking on its website) are ripe to help your signage both engage and inform.

My point is that there is so much that is interesting and informative about this product (and others), but most of the stores I visit use nondescript signage highlighting names and trumpeting prices. Usually, it's the same old thing! I suggest, as a good rule of thumb, to try to only mention facts that aren't easily discerned by picking up a bottle. Teach the consumer something.

I'd even consider using the *Wall Street Journal's* quote about Tito's: "America's first craft sippin' vodka". Putting these words on a sign would help to capitalize on the craft brew phenomenon sweeping the country and might very well cause a consumer to stop and pick up a bottle.

Just because the Tito's (and other similarly displayed products) occupies prime real estate doesn't mean that consumers will stop and purchase. Shoppers are moving faster and faster these days. It's not hard to imagine someone blowing right by a big stack of product without noticing its sign. As it is, most signs get just 2 seconds of time with the average consumer, which makes the message even more important.

Engage by way of capturing attention, and inform by way of teaching something about the product. Get your creative juices flowing, but remember that simplicity is the best approach. Don't obscure the message with fancy color themes, overwhelming language, or breathtaking graphics.

And managers have a big role in this…

…Which is why I categorize this as a mistake smart managers <u>don't</u> make! Simply, if managers don't instill the need for better in-store merchandising, then it will never happen. If managers don't help sales professionals and other associates see the importance of maximizing every merchandising opportunity, then products will never be promoted to their fullest potential.

So, make every effort to engage and inform, and consumers will pay more attention. Your products, (once consumers learn their amazing stories), will be purchased in droves.

You might have to build a new display!

That's just the way it works.

MISTAKE 3

APPEARING "HO-HUM" ABOUT YOUR PRODUCTS

Is it possible to be too gung-ho about your products? Said another way, can you ever be too ho-hum about your products? If your associates would rather be selling Cubs World Series clothing, or anything other than your products, will your customers be able to tell? Will they know?

That's a trick question: World Series Clothing for the Cubs. There is no such thing! But really, how does enthusiasm play into the purchase equation?

Our trip to the Honda dealer may shine some light on that.

Recently, our family purchased a new Honda Accord. My son Josh went with me to pick up the car, and while we waited to sign the papers, one of the dealership's veterans discussed the car's ownership kit with us.

As Josh and I watched, Henry waxed poetic about the car's ownership kit. It was bizarre, almost scary. I've never seen someone so excited to tell us that if we didn't want to read the *whole owner's manual*, we could read the *summary owner's manual*. He took such pleasure in telling us how to open the trunk. Clearly, he wanted to make sure we were comfortable with the new car, but after a while, his broad smile started freaking us out.

After we finally extricated ourselves from Henry's grip, Josh expressed what his glances had already told me.

"What's up with that guy?"

But Henry's outward enthusiasm got me thinking. Is there such a thing as being too gung-ho about your products? To be sure, Henry probably likes Honda automobiles. Perhaps he even loves Honda automobiles and his job and the dealer for which he works. The difference between Henry and others who claim to love their products is that his enthusiasm seemed genuine and real.

Before I go on, let me ask if you're a wee bit confused. At the beginning of the chapter, I described Henry's demeanor "as freaking me out a bit." Now, I'm saying that his enthusiasm seemed genuine and real. Am I contradicting myself? Absolutely not! His attitude was infectious, just a bit over the top. Maybe he needed to tone it down a notch.

But please don't misunderstand! I'd much rather have infectious enthusiasm, even if it's a bit hokey, over someone who is ho-hum about his or her products. That's a big mistake in my book and the type of behavior we (as managers) have to watch for very closely in our people.

Now that I've cleared that up, let me ask you the most important question.

Can your customers tell how you (and your associates) think and feel about your company and its products?

Is your enthusiasm noticeable? Is it infectious? Is it real?

To be genuine and effective, enthusiasm must be infectious and real, and not necessarily in that order!

First, enthusiasm has to be real and genuine. That is, if your enthusiasm is manufactured, your customers will know. To see my point, consider the following questions:

Do you have to love your products? Not necessarily. Do you have to like your products? Not really.

Do you have to possess a real belief that your products will make your customers money?

Absolutely. And you must convey this to your customers.

Second, enthusiasm must be infectious. You can believe with every breath that your brands are the real deal, but if you're not able to transfer this feeling to your customers, your belief isn't worth a hill of beans. Selling is the transference of your feelings for your products to your customers. Back in the day, I had many sales professionals sit in front of me showing that they couldn't care less about what was "in the bag" that day. Many of these professionals looked like they were about to board the Titanic... after it began sinking!

The face a customer sees should not resemble your latest mug shot.

Or your expression as your dentist gets the drill ready.

But, really, absent any level of enthusiasm, I was hardly ever moved to purchase.

I figured if they don't care, why should I care?

I didn't buy that day and, given similar circumstances, neither will your customers — today or any other day.

That's just the way it works.

MISTAKE 4

ASSUMING PEOPLE ARE LISTENING

I was recently asked the following question:

"What do you make of the following situation? My sales professional failed to execute in an important account and we ended up with *egg on our faces* with the supplier. I was very clear in laying out what was expected; I even prepared a handout and mentioned the supplier visit (and the related to-do items) in a sales meeting. I don't understand why simple instructions, like making sure a store has a display, proper signage and adequate cooler representation are so hard to follow.

Am I doing something wrong?"

Here's my answer.

Sounds like your team really *laid an egg*. Your culpability depends on exactly what you did to give your sales professional the best chance to meet your expectations. Before we go any further, let me first say that I understand how frustrating it can be to have to motivate (even pressure) people to follow simple instructions. Reminds me of raising my boys and how hard it can be getting them to do what they know they need to do. (Danny, have you made your bed today?)

I like your question because it indicates that you're willing to examine your own actions. Too many managers look the other way. Let's face it – it's much easier to say, "I've discovered the problem: it's you!" than to accept personal accountability. Including yourself in the accountability equation is a strong leadership move on your part and will pay great dividends in the future.

As you probably know, the first step is to set clear expectations. It sounds like you did, but I have one question for you. Do you know if your sales professional read the handout or was paying attention during the sales meeting? One of the biggest mistakes managers make in conveying expectations is to assume that 1) they are being heard and 2) the intended target of their words is noting what is being said. It's not the same thing. Hearing you is good, but making a note with an attached action step is much better altogether.

So what we have here is a basketful of assumptions. For the best possible execution, don't assume that your people will fill in the blanks. Don't assume that because they've executed in the past, they're going to follow through this time. Don't assume that you were clear enough, because you may not have been. Don't assume that people are listening or the *yoke* will be on you!

The second step is to offer support. Doesn't seem like there is much opportunity for that here, but if you could have provided merchandising or other related help, I hope you did so.

The third step would have prevented you from getting egg on your face. Did you check for understanding? In other words, did you ensure that your sales professional read the handout or was paying attention the numerous times the expectation was mentioned?

You're probably thinking, isn't this simple execution what we pay people to do? Why should I have to do this? It's a good question, and one upon which many management books are written.

I'll give you an un-sophisticated answer.

Because you have to.

When you have a key expectation, one for which there will be severe repercussions if the team fails, then it makes all the sense in the world to check that your professional understands the game plan; that he or she understands what to do and is committed to doing it.

During your team meeting, in as positive a tone as possible, go around the table to gauge everyone's grasp of the key expectation. Say, "Tom, are we on the same page with the XYZ account? Great! What is your next action step?" Wrap it up by saying, "Are there any reasons for me to expect that this task won't be accomplished?" Have your sales professionals respond verbally, much like passengers in the emergency row of an airplane are asked to actually say yes when asked if they understand the flight attendant's instructions. (Yes, despite my relative lack of height, I need the extra legroom!)

The key is to ferret out all the excuses ahead of time.

So where did it all go wrong?

The train might have derailed at any time, but there was one major mistake that smart managers don't make. The mistake was assuming that the sales professional was listening. That he received the message. That his elevator made it to the top floor that day. That he wasn't a few feet short of the runway…

I could go on.

Checking would have kept your face egg-free!

So – next time be more specific and check for understanding. You'll be glad you did, as will the supplier because…

That's just the way it works. (On second thought, is the supplier ever really satisfied?)

MISTAKE 5

AVOIDING DIFFICULT CONVERSATIONS

We have sump-pump issues at the Rosen household. Why we have six of them and why they all need servicing at the same time, well, that's a subject for a different day.

Recently, an engineer came out to the house to explain some options to Jill and I, and, of course, the explanation went way over my head.

I should explain.

See, I don't have a scientific mind. I never have.

It reminded me of the results of my first physics exam, sophomore year at Indiana University. I earned a 12%, which is 3 correct answers out of 25, for those of you keeping score at home. I guess I thought "no charge" was when you get a free drink, not the difference between a proton and a neutron.

I remember how I moseyed right over to the registrar's office after this happened and dropped the class – like a bad habit. My buddies knew, but my parents... well, they were left in the dark on that one.

It was so much easier then! Quickly and painlessly dropping a thorn from my side.

Is that what you do when you have a difficult situation with someone on your team?

Do you avoid the (thorn) individual and "drop the class," if you will? Is that even an option?

My guess would be no and no, that you're not that lucky. Further, I gather that you probably have to face uncomfortable situations in work and life almost every day.

I dropped physics that year. Consider the following, and you'll have more positive discussions when things get challenging.

1.   Check within.

When I say "check within," I'm suggesting that you look inward at your own actions and behaviors. To illustrate my point, do you ever watch NBC's Law and Order? Do you ever notice how each interrogation room has a window? From a different room, the detectives can look through the window and see the suspect. However, if the suspect looks through the same window, all he or she sees is a mirror of his or her reflection.

Do you look through a window or a mirror?

Our mindset is that it's so much easier to blame someone else for our difficulties, to look through a window, if you will. To see the other person as a victim and to feel helpless in the matter.

Managers who handle sensitive matters productively look through a mirror. They check to see what, if anything, they have to do with the problem and then take corrective action. As I've said in other parts of this book, rarely are we innocent bystanders in the dramas we find ourselves in. Sadly, we're often the lead actor!

2.   Speak in facts, not opinions.

The first 30 seconds of a conversation are crucial. Often, this short period will determine success or failure. Start with facts (or questions), not opinions. Facts (while certainly disputable) are much safer. Saying "Why were you late?" is much wiser than saying, "The fact that you were late tells me that you don't value your job!" The latter statement will start a wildfire. The former will give you a chance. Think questions, not statements.

3.   Look at the specific situation.

Watch out for what behaviorists call the *fundamental attribution error*, in which one assumes that others act in a certain way because it's in their make-up or because they enjoy acting that way. We look at one's activities in a dispositional way, rather than in a situational way. In other words, we automatically assume that one's actions reflect their character, as opposed to what happened in a specific situation. We overstate the bad in people and see the other as a villain, instead of as a reasonable person.

Just because Frank is late for work doesn't mean he doesn't value his job.

4.   Align your mutual purposes.

Let the other person know that you're aiming for a scenario that brings a mutually beneficial outcome. Undoubtedly, if you're a manager (embroiled in a challenging situation), then you may be dealing with an individual who feels threatened. Letting the person know that you both have the same mutual purpose will help alleviate his or her stress. Some sort of partnership statement will make it safe for others to hear what you have to say. For example, say, "As we're both in this together, let's brainstorm a few ways to improve our selling skills as we head into the new year. I'll support you any way I can. Does that sound like a plan?"

This statement stresses the future and suggests that you're there to support your associate. It also aims for a little buy-in from your associate, and that will go a long way.

5.   Show respect.

Watch your gestures and mannerisms. If your arms are folded and you're rolling your eyes and interrupting constantly, no amount of "I value your opinion" is going to rise above that behavior. Make sure to consider what your body language says about your intentions.

6.   Give yourself a timeout.

Be patient if the conversation gets heated. As you probably know, emotions unleash a flood of unproductive chemicals into the body that influence behavior and actions. Once these chemicals are released, they hang around in the bloodstream for a while. It may take some time before you can continue your conversation. Often, it's best to let negative situations run off your back. Excuse yourself if you have to. Give yourself a timeout. Get a drink of water or a bite to eat. Take a break! Do anything to clear your head.

7.   Prepare.

Perhaps you've noticed a theme here. Put simply, you can avoid a plethora of conversational mistakes by preparing. Take the time to outline what you want to say. When I coach managers prior to a difficult conversation, we focus on how to frame the situation and get the conversation started in a positive manner. We also spend time considering what kinds of responses we might get. This way, there is a plan in place. It's not perfect, but it's better than winging it!

With a plan in place, there is a much greater likelihood for success. Never choose the certainty of a bad situation over the uncertainty of addressing a difficult situation head-on.

Don't make the mistake of assuming the problem will go away. Your sump-pump might take the water away, but problem situations don't drain that easily.

That's just the way it works!

MISTAKE 6

BLINDSIDING YOUR PEOPLE

Over the last several years, I've been fortunate to work with many managers. Some are middle managers in sales organizations, while others manage retail stores. Before any coaching takes place, I have a preliminary conversation with a manager at the senior level so I can develop a list of skill sets to concentrate on with the person I'm coaching.

A few weeks back, my assignment was to help Tom improve in a few key areas. To prepare, I met with Shelia to discuss where to focus my attention.

She wanted Tom work on…

1)   Preparing for his weekly team meetings more diligently,
2)   Organizing his day-to-day activities more efficiently, and
3)   Improving his communication, specifically when having to address his team's areas of improvement.

When Tom and I sat down, I posed the following question: "Tom, in what areas would Shelia like to see you improve?"

Tom thought for a nanosecond before replying, "Shelia wants me to get out in the field more!"

I asked Tom again and he shared the same answer.

This seemed like a major disconnect to me.

Unfortunately, it's a dynamic I see all too often. Managers simply aren't candid enough with their people. As a result, they end up blindsiding their people with the truth, often during a performance review. (We'll get to that in a second.)

A manager's inability to be completely honest typically stems from the usual laundry list of reasons.

For example, perhaps Shelia is afraid of confrontation. She may be reluctant to bring up subjects that she knows from past experience will raise Tom's defenses. Maybe she's worried about negatively affecting Tom's morale. She may not want to upset the applecart, so to speak. Or what if she believes that she hasn't supported Tom strategically, or done enough to help him be successful?

That last reason would certainly make it more difficult for Shelia to level with Tom.

Through my coaching, I've noticed that many managers have these fears and, as a result, people like Tom are often left in the dark on how to improve. In fact, I find that nearly 70% of sales professionals and other associates know that their work needs improvement, but they're not sure a) which areas need work, and b) how to go about improving.

Talk about not knowing which way is up!

As I considered the dynamic between Tom and Shelia, I came to the conclusion that Tom (like many before him) knew that his performance was in need of improvement, but wasn't sure what to do.

I was getting the feeling Shelia hadn't been so truthful after all.

After coaching Tom, I placed a call to Shelia. I related his comments and then asked Shelia, "Does he know where you want to see improvement?"

"Oh yeah, he knows. We talked about it at his last performance review."

That was almost 8 months ago.

Maybe you're thinking, "What's wrong with using the performance review to examine areas for improvement?"

Well, nothing – just as long as the performance review conversation is combined with other weekly or monthly conversations. Let's be real for a moment. Performance reviews are a tricky proposition. For starters, the performance review represents a bit of a "verdict" for the recipient. It's like the jury has already decided the outcome –in the past tense. To make matters worse, the recipient is likely to attend the meeting with a nervous and defensive posture because the situation is particularly nerve-racking. Making matters worse, everyone is waiting at home to hear how it went!

It's not the time to introduce something new; there should be no surprises. In fact, besides communicating financial specifics and goals, etc., there really shouldn't be any new ground to cover. Nobody should be blindsided. Especially Tom.

Tom's areas of improvement should be the subjects in most, if not all of their one-to-one conversations throughout the year. Shelia should be carefully questioning Tom to ascertain how he's doing in these areas. She should also be observing Tom in action to see how he's progressing. This should be an activity that takes place throughout the year, not just on special occasions.

Should Shelia be blunt in her conversations with him?

Well, I'm not sure I like the word blunt in this case, but my hope is for Shelia to have the guts to tell Tom the truth in an honest, straightforward way. Note: being honest doesn't mean being rude. It doesn't mean being negative, petty or trivial. It means sharing the truth in as positive a manner as possible.

Being rude and honest are two different things entirely. (I wish my college girlfriend had known this, but that's not the point.)

The word "rude" is defined (according to dictionary.com) as *being discourteous or impolite, especially in a deliberate way.* Being honest is defined as *being honorable in principles, intentions and actions.* If we examine the two definitions closely, we can reasonably say that being rude is deliberate, while honesty is manifested through one's intentions. So, if your intention is to aid improvement, then honesty is good. If your goal is to knock someone down a notch or two deliberately, then you should probably work on a more positive way to convey your thoughts. I'd start working on that today!

I bristle when I hear a manager tell me that he had to "lay into so and so," because it shouldn't be that way. That type of activity is ego-driven. It's more for the benefit of the manager than it is for the person on the receiving end.

Smart managers don't make that mistake. I suppose I could have made *being rude* mistake 51 — but I digress.

Let's go back to Tom and Shelia. Tom genuinely wanted the truth about his performance.

Do your people want to know the truth?

I believe so. Most of the professionals I talk with want candor. They want to hear the truth, especially in these tough economic times; as jobs are so scarce and most want to hold on to the one they have. No one wants to live in delusion and fantasy — as wonderful as these locales may seem — only to be blindsided with a menu of their weaknesses when it's too late to correct them.

The naked truth, while not always easy to see or hear, promotes trust and respect.

The key is to do it in as positive a manner as possible.

Let's go back to Shelia and Tom as we wrap up this chapter. I imagine Tom is at least vaguely aware of Shelia's list of improvements; I'm not suggesting that they never discuss these issues. For maximum results, though, these improvements should be the source of continual conversations between the two of them. If Tom had sat down and said, "I'm supposed to plan better team meetings, be more organized and improve my communication skills," then I would have been more comfortable. I would have seen that Shelia was coaching Tom in a consistent, continual way with no intention of blindsiding him at the annual performance review.

It takes frequent candor for that to happen… and once a year simply doesn't get the job done.

That's just the way it works.

MISTAKE 7

BUILDING CONNECTIONS 140 CHARACTERS AT A TIME

Do you and your associates ever use old-fashioned methods to build rapport?

I hope so – as you'll soon see.

Better question: are you taking advantage of opportunities as they present themselves? Are your people? Are your professionals building rapport?

This chapter pertains to anyone who interacts with customers and all managers who coach and lead their teams in the pursuit of strong execution and bountiful sales results.

It shouldn't be a great surprise that the subject is my love for the Cubs!

Everybody who knows me understands that I am a die-hard, long-suffering, perpetually disappointed (almost dead inside) Chicago Cubs baseball fan. In my old office (in Chicago) were at least 50 pictures taken at Cubs games, including many photos from my August 2003 trip to Wrigley Field. Yes, the Cubs lost that day (what else is new?), but before the game, my wife and my two older sons had the opportunity to meet two players, Kerry Wood and Mark Prior, in the dugout. Oddly enough, they weren't on the DL that day!

In those days, my boys were into the Cubbies – for 15 minutes anyway. They quickly got off that train to nowhere leaving me to suffer by my lonesome… But I digress.

Anyway, everybody who visited my office knew about my weakness for the Cubbies. This included Frank, a sales professional whose business never went very far with us. He never made any real effort to connect. One day, while at Wrigley (and witnessing another losing effort), I saw Frank. And after seeing how he was dressed, my jaw just about hit the floor.

Frank was dressed in Cubbie blue from head to toe. He wore baseball shoes. Not sure if they had spikes, but they certainly were blue. He had on pinstripe baseball pants, a blue belt, a mock turtleneck with a Cubs emblem, a regulation jersey and a Cubs hat. He was really decked out. To be honest, it was kind of creepy.

It should come as no surprise that there wasn't a significant other with him.

All I could say was, "Frank, why didn't you tell me?" I was shocked almost to the point of not being able to say anything, which is unusual for me. Frank missed such a huge opportunity to connect with me on a more personal level.

So what happened after that day at Wrigley?

We became friends and went to numerous games in Chicago.

Can you guess what happened to his sales? Why, yes, they increased.

And when Frank took me to an away playoff game in Florida (separate rooms, thank you very much), you can probably guess what happened after that. Why, yes, his sales increased yet again.

Just a quick aside at this juncture – Frank was strongly dissuaded (with the loss of all my business) from wearing a head-to-toe Cubs uniform ever while I was present.

I just wanted to get that right out there.

Now, please understand – this is not a story about buying a customer's business, although I did enjoy the playoff game. It's more about putting yourself in a better position to seize the day with customers or associates alike.

Think about it this way. Baseball games aren't exactly bastions of excitement. What were Frank and I talking about during pitching changes and the numerous other stoppages in play? Sure, we talked about the game, but we also talked about my business. We talked about his products.

And what did we talk about during the scoreboard race?

We talked about my goals. We talked about what I valued in a business partner.

Most importantly, we talked about how his products would help my business. By the way, how come the doughnut always wins. You'd think the bagel would win once in a while. Must be all that cream cheese. Or the energy bar...

Anyway, Frank and I began building rapport the old-fashioned way – hence my question at the beginning of this chapter. We didn't trade emails, send texts, write on each other's Facebook walls or tweet each other.

We didn't even use Skype.

No, we sat face-to-face and I shared my *status* the old-fashioned way. I saw the conviction in his eyes when it came to his products and how genuinely he felt that his portfolio would help my business. And he was right. Doing business with Frank did benefit me more than I had ever imagined.

So, as you navigate through the new style of communication, make sure that you and your associates don't forget what some would call the prehistoric way of communication. You simply can't get to know someone in 140 characters or less.

That's just the way it works!

MISTAKE 8

COMMUNICATING UNCLEARLY

Have you heard of Amelia Bedelia?

Amelia Bedelia is a character from a series of children's books. Her character (a housekeeper) takes everything literally and usually to comical extremes. I remember reading the books to my children when they were younger. Amelia always needed explicit instructions, or things went wrong. Very wrong! For example, if you said, "Steal home plate," in the midst of a baseball game, Amelia would literally take home plate and run away with it. If she made a sponge cake, she put real sponges in the cake. If she was asked to "put the lights out," she actually hung the light bulbs out on a clothesline!

You get the picture. It's pretty funny stuff, actually. Hey… *The Cat in the Hat* got old after a while!

Out of left field recently (pun intended), Amelia's name was brought up by one of my managers.

We were discussing the act of setting and communicating expectations. As I often do, I was imploring the managers to be explicit with their people to increase productivity and reduce needless misunderstandings. One manager referenced Amelia Bedelia and asked if he needed to be that clear…

Did he have to spell things out with similar clarity and redundancy, like they had to for Amelia Bedelia after all of her hilarious escapades?

Did he need to be that clear and concise with his associates, even if it was obvious?

I didn't answer right away.

Instead, I asked the managers one by one, "Do tasks have a higher chance of being accomplished when you're more explicit?"

Most nodded or said, "Yes."

"Does execution in your accounts improve when you share more details?"

"Yes."

"Do misunderstandings decrease when you check for understanding to make sure that your people are clear on your wishes?"

"Yes."

"It seems like babysitting," one of the guys muttered. From the looks of the others, I could tell many agreed with that statement.

I couldn't disagree. It does seem like babysitting, and I do know this. If you set clear expectations, though, and offer your support and check for understanding, you will leave much less to chance.

And there will be fewer mistakes.

That's just the way it works!

MISTAKE 9

DELAYING THE TRUTH

The Theo Epstein era has gotten off to a quick start here in Chicago.

Shortly after Epstein took office, the new Cubs president fired the current manager, Mike Quade, and ruled out the one manager clamored for by most all Cubs fans.

Yes, I'm referring to Hall of Fame second baseman Ryne Sandberg, who had a distinguished career in Chicago. He was quickly ruled out as a possibility of being the next Cubs' manager because he didn't have any major league coaching experience.

The Cubs didn't even interview him.

Shortly after the current manager was fired, the Cubs' new management team put in a phone call to Sandberg. (Note: They didn't call his agent, nor did they send a text or an email. They called him directly. More on that later.)

The candor or the up-front way they handled the situation was beautiful!

Theo knew Cubs fans would demand that the club consider their beloved "Ryno". Instead of letting him (Ryno) twist in the wind, Theo let everyone know up front (including Ryno) that they were going in a different direction.

Perhaps that direction will include winning a few playoff games. Is that asking so much from a franchise whose last World Series title came four years before the Titanic sank?

Anyway, in notifying Sandberg as they did, the Cubs did the right thing and the fair thing.

Not only did they not have to address consistent Ryno rumors (which could have hampered their efforts to bring in a quality manager), but they also left him free to interview for other jobs without the specter of the Cub's opening hanging over his head. Their bad news actually did him a favor, although it might not have seemed that way at the time.

The Cub's new level of transparency and honesty is refreshing, and we can all learn from it. If you ask yourself the questions below, your answers will help you be perceived as more credible with associates, customers, and whomever else you deal with.

• Do you demonstrate ownership and a sense of urgency?

Your associates and customers want a quick turnaround when they have a problem or concern, not the runaround!

• Are you clear on when you will respond?

If a problem or concern does occur, communicate — as quickly as possible — the details on how you will fix the issue and how you will ensure that it does not occur again. Responsiveness builds credibility, which leads to trust. By the way, one of my biggest regrets in business is not responding to my people faster on vacation requests. I was such a weenie!

I know they wanted to book "super-saver" fares and such, and I fear my foot-dragging cost a few dollars, or more, for the very people I claimed to value so much. For matters of personal importance, make sure to respond quickly or, at the very least, share *when* you will respond.

• Do you return calls and emails promptly?

Return calls and emails promptly, especially if you've made a mistake. No hiding behind voicemail! No hiding, period!

• Do you hide behind email?

Speaking of playing hide and seek, many professionals tell me that their managers hide behind email, especially when any element of conflict is involved. According to the Harvard Business Review, "The biggest drawback and danger with email is that the tone and context are easy to misread. In a live conversation, how one says something, with modulations and intonations, is as important as what they are saying. With email, it's hard to get the feelings behind the words."

But you probably know that. Perhaps you already learned that lesson the hard way.

There is no question that electronic communication has revolutionized the way we communicate. Unfortunately, these mediums are decreasing the rate at which people are willing to resolve issues face-to-face.

It might not seem so, because some people will say anything via email; but when you're trying to put your best foot forward and resolve issues, hiding behind emails won't do you any favors. Further, I find that email prolongs debate. I've also seen discussions start out as just that, discussions; only to escalate to conflict because of misinterpretations.

It's always best to meet face-to-face.

• **Are you open, candid, and transparent?**

Ask yourself: Am I withholding information that I should be sharing? Am I forcing others to ask for the truth? Am I an open book or a closed book? Do people trust me?

• **Do you earn trust or ask for it?**

Never say, "Trust me!" Either they do or they don't, and asking for it won't help. Build credibility with your actions. That will help you more than anything else.

• **Do you follow through like you said you would?**

Did you say you would do something? Keep your word! Never make your customer beg for information to sell your products.

• **Do you admit your mistakes?**

Are you accountable for your actions? Nothing destroys credibility more than those who blame everyone else but have a hard time pointing the finger inward.

• **Do you restate commitments?**

It's much better to verify and be sure then to have the customer turn the truck away because they never agreed to anything!

Let's go back to the Cubs and Theo Epstein again for a brief moment as we conclude this chapter.

Because of the candor and honesty, everybody in this situation came out a winner. Even Mike Quade, the fired manager, emerged pretty well, as he wasn't left to ponder his fate any longer. Plus, he gets a cool million for the second year of his contract, which is good money for taking a year off to go fishing. Plus, he got to escape the Cubs! That's priceless, as the commercial goes. I should only be so lucky...

Usually everyone wins except for the Cubs, but hopefully, this will change under the new regime.

And if the early returns are any indication, their treatment of sensitive situations will create an environment where talented baseball players and professionals (scouts, etc.) work diligently to build a consistent winner.

The same will be true for you, as long as you don't hide the truth.

That's just the way it works!

MISTAKE 10

DISPENSING TOO MUCH ADVICE

Do you know someone who always has an answer for you?

And it doesn't matter what you're asking, he or she pipes in with an answer whether you want it or not?

Is the answer *usually* correct? Better question: Is the answer *ever* correct?

You know, like a mother-in-law or similar relative always chiming with an untimely opinion? (Not my mother-in-law, mind you; other people's mother-in-laws...)

But, seriously, have you ever been accused of giving too much advice?

Of being a bit too much like Dr. Phil?

I've come across numerous managers who enjoy sharing advice and not too long ago I met a middle manager named Larry who fit the mold perfectly. Back when I met Larry, he dispensed advice as if he was a vending machine and my challenge was to get him to give less advice, so his people could (and would) solve more problems and create more opportunities on their own.

Larry meant well, but he was really having a rough time. As I observed him coaching Pete, I noticed that every chance he could, he'd jump in to tell Pete exactly how to handle whatever needed to be handled. Pete never had a chance, and you could see that he (Pete) was a bit put-off by the whole scene. He felt dejected, demoralized, and de-motivated.

Not exactly what Larry was looking for in this situation.

And Pete isn't alone. Many associates with advice-giving, overbearing bosses feel as Pete does.

Larry, the manager, isn't alone either.

I've had several managers/performance coaches confide in me that they are habitual advice-givers. Sure, they know that it's important to teach a man to fish, but, instead, they give the whole school away just for the asking. Why? Because that's what managers do. They solve problems. They're there for their people. Plus, managers are usually pressed for time, and giving the solution is much easier (and more time efficient) than having the patience to coach people to find solutions on their own.

But is giving advice as productive as helping people learn to handle what comes their way?

Well, no!

If you're a performance sales coach (and I presume you're striving for higher performance), then your objective is to help your professionals solve their own problems. Your role is to help your professionals make decisions — increasingly complex decisions, as a matter of fact. Your goal is to teach your professionals to act on their own and to move from needing you more to needing you less.

And that's an uncomfortable place for many managers — to be needed less.

Most managers' intentions are pure. They want to help. Maybe there is some ego involved, but it's more from the standpoint of being needed. Sure, some want to solve all the problems because it makes them feel better about themselves (and look better to others), but not all managers.

The problem is, when a manager like Larry jumps in, he creates more dependency. In this case, there's a little resentment, especially when the recommended solution doesn't work.

Further, when managers give advice, they become the problem-solver, and associates like Pete are no longer part of the solution. Because Larry solves Pete's problems, Pete learns absolutely nothing about problem solving. No strategies or other skills for moving the ball forward.

Check that. He'll learn how to be more dependent on others. It's a vicious circle.

Ironically, one of Larry's questions for me was why Pete (and others) came to him incessantly for help. I asked him, "When people come to you, what do you usually say?"

"I give the answer to get them out of my hair!"

I asked him, "By giving advice so readily, is there really any reason to figure anything out, despite the negative feelings that come along as a result?"

Larry figured, in the long run, it was just easier for Pete to take the help. Plus, maybe he (Larry) was sending a signal that he actually wanted to field questions. He did want to help, just not all the time.

He realized the error of his ways.

My suggestion for Larry also goes for anybody faced with an advice-seeker. The next time you're asked for help, try the following scenario instead.

Say, "What do you think?" Then listen for the wisdom to spill out. If they say, "I don't know..." don't take the bait. Instead say, "What would it be if you did know?" If they say, "What do you think?" turn the tables and say, "What do you think?" It may seem argumentative at first, but after one or two times, they won't ask anymore. They'll take more initiative to figure things out on their own, because your help isn't so accessible.

And that's a good thing. Yes, lending support is also good. Answering questions and being a resource is good. Following up is good. But doing all the heavy lifting, thus absolving Pete from that burden, isn't an ideal solution. It's not any solution – period.

Always ask – *Is what I'm about to do (or say) going to help develop my associate or sales professional?* By considering your actions in this manner, you'll ascertain whether you're helping your people or holding them back.

When asking questions, take your time, but let your associates know that you expect an answer. Engage them in conversations about solutions and opportunities. They'll be better off for it, and so will you.

That's just the way it works.

MISTAKE 11

DOUSING IDEAS WITH A FIRE HOSE

Do you solicit your associates' ideas?

Do you create an environment where your people can (and will) share their ideas?

Do you facilitate an atmosphere where people can share their thoughts without fear of ridicule?

Do you douse ideas with a fire hose?

This chapter is all about the practice known as brainstorming and we'll get to good facilitator skills (and dousing ideas) in a moment.

Before we get started, let's discuss the basics. Brainstorming seems easy enough – doesn't it? Just get everybody together with a topic and have at it - right?

Well, not exactly!

A few weeks ago I was asked to observe a brainstorming session for a client. It was decent, for the facilitator's first try, and we can learn a lot from his effort.

There was room for improvement and that's a good thing, because soliciting your associates' ideas is a great area for you to improve your skills.

Perhaps the main reason why brainstorming can fail is because of poor facilitation. In other words, the facilitator (or manager) doesn't manage the time properly, doesn't keep focus on the topic at hand and allows common breaches of etiquette.

The great news is that if the facilitator improves in these areas (and just a few others), brainstorming exercises can be a great way to solicit employee involvement. The more your people feel their contributions are wanted, the better.

Consider the following as you start to use brainstorming to spice up your meetings and make the mutual creation of ideas a core part of your company culture:

- **Good facilitators push idea generation, not idea evaluation.**

The purpose of brainstorming is not analyzing ideas. The purpose is idea generation. There is always time for evaluation and analysis after the fact. Good facilitators keep the scope specific and encourage as many suggestions as possible that fit those terms. Good facilitators include detail about the desired outcome and, consequently, the ideas are more targeted and more relevant. Most of all, good facilitators foster an environment where everyone's ideas are accepted. There is no fire hosing (or spraying water on other's ideas) as I've heard it called. With this strict control, everyone is actively encouraged (and more likely) to participate.

Let's expand on this concept of fire hosing for moment. I'd like to explain why I consider this important enough to include as a chapter in this book.

The concept of sharing one's opinion reminds me of listening to sports talk radio. Often, especially around a sport's trading deadline, callers will suggest the most bizarre trades. If sports talk radio was around in 1964, I'm sure a caller would have outlandishly suggested that the Cubs should Lou Brock to the Cardinals for Ernie Broglio. The Cubs would never make that trade. (Oh, wait. They did make that trade. What a *smart* trade! It only took the Cards a few months to win the World Series. The Cubs? It's been more than a few months. Slightly.)

How many bases did Lou Brock steal?

Anyway, the point is that many people are inherently opinionated and, as such, they want to share their opinions – no matter the substance of said opinion. And I've learned over time that your employees don't necessarily expect you to *act* on their ideas, but they do want you to *hear* their ideas.

Great managers don't ridicule (or douse) their associates' ideas.

- **Good facilitators understand time management.**

Good facilitators set the ground rules from the start and a critical skill is deciding how time will be spent. The goal is to maintain interest. First, set a time limit for idea generation. Second, set aside time to review ideas and ask for explanations. Please note: this only takes place after everyone has had a chance to contribute. For maximum productivity, a good facilitator should ask attendees to come prepared with three ideas to get the ball rolling. Finally, after everyone has contributed and everyone is clear on the ideas, time should be allocated to specify next steps, which might include some fact-finding and analysis on all the available choices. Make sure to let people know that they can text in or otherwise share ideas later. Good ideas can appear at all hours, not just during your pre-assigned brainstorming sessions.

- **Good facilitators keep the group focused.**

In the session I observed, the facilitator didn't take enough time to communicate the desired outcome – new, fresh ideas to help move a languishing product. As a result, there were some pretty "out there" ideas and many attendees jumped on the tangent bandwagon for suggestions that didn't answer or even come close to addressing the subject at hand.

I'm not saying that they weren't good ideas – they just weren't relevant. A good facilitator makes it perfectly clear what the problem or question up for debate is so that suggestions and ideas are pertinent. This practice lends more productivity to the process. And if the group gets sidetracked, instead of knocking people down a rung or two, a good facilitator re-directs the conversation while keeping track of worthy topics for future sessions.

- **Good facilitators maintain proper etiquette.**

In other words, a good facilitator prevents people from talking over each other. A good facilitator keeps people in line. A good facilitator understands that laughter and sarcasm might not seem outwardly harmful, but also realizes that you won't get many suggestions from the laughed-at individual in the future. A good facilitator makes it safe for everyone to contribute and goes out of his or her way to encourage the quiet and reserved types, since it's not just the blowhards that have something to contribute. No offense to the blowhards. You know who you are.

So there you have it. Four ideas for better brainstorming sessions. After you facilitate a successful session, don't forget to follow up. Besides poor facilitation, the other attribute I've noticed with poor brainstorming sessions is that nothing happens afterwards. The ideas aren't acted upon; it's like the session never happened.

So, if you want to kill idea generation in your business, just ignore or otherwise table good ideas and suggestions from your brainstorming sessions. Pull the fire alarm and douse ideas (both good or bad) with the entire capacity of your town's municipal water supply. You won't have to worry about such contributions in the future because there won't be any!

That's just the way it works.

.

MISTAKE 12

DUMPING DATA

During your weekly meeting, do you ever feel like you're at the local landfill?

Let me ask this question another way.

Do you use meetings to routinely dump mounds of facts, features, goals and inventory levels on your team? Do your meetings exist solely for the purpose of disseminating information, or is there some interaction built into the agenda?

Once in a while I'll ask professionals to share what they do to liven up their meetings. A majority of the answers have something to do with less information and more interaction.

Other times, I have a team of managers who feel strongly about spending any available time disseminating information. These managers feel that they have too much information to share and discuss, so finding a few minutes to incorporate more interaction simply isn't possible.

I had such a team not too long ago. They felt that going over inventory levels and discussing deals was all they had time for. We went back and forth for a bit and I wasn't able to convince them otherwise.

Before we go any further, let me explain that I understand the need to convey information in a timely manner. Certainly, sending uninformed professionals out into the field isn't wise. However, there are other ways to convey information and, more importantly, when the team gets together, there is the potential for much greater benefit.

Start moving towards more interactive meetings by taking baby steps. If your meeting is usually 60 minutes, replace 10 minutes of data dumping with an interactive exercise (such as the following) with the express purpose of exchanging ideas. This is the area where I think the most improvement can be made, and I'm surprised more sales managers don't incorporate this type of interaction.

Start with a blank sheet of flip chart paper and introduce one new item. You can also use a difficult-to-sell item. It doesn't really matter. Go around the room soliciting suggestions and strategies on how to sell that item.

Identify reasons as to why customers should be interested. Provide answers to the question, "Who cares?" Grab as many ideas as possible. Push back hard on weak (or phony) attributes. This exercise not only keeps your team engaged, but also provides them with new tools that will enable them to succeed better than a "how was your weekend" portion of the meeting would.

Additionally, for more engaging and interactive meetings, ask yourself the following questions: (If any of the answers are no, then you know what to work on. Liven it up a bit.)

- Would my team come to the weekly meeting if it were optional?
- Does every member of my team leave the meeting with a new idea to try or a new skill to practice?
- Do I share too much material in too little time?
- Do I spend too much time with my back to the team? (In other words, am I just reading off PowerPoint slides?)
- Do I let meetings go past the announced ending time?
- Do we get mired in details that are better off discussed with individuals?
- Am I preparing enough for the meeting?
- Am I communicating what I expect from my attendees?
- Am I following an agenda that clearly states a few desired outcomes? (Has anyone even seen the agenda?)
- Am I scheduling others into the agenda? (Nothing wakes people up quicker than a part in the play!)
- Am I standing up and/or moving around enough to stimulate attention?
- Am I including everyone in the group? (Am I making sure that the shy types are being heard?)
- Am I telling stories in such a way as to capture minds and hearts?
- Am I using hand gestures and other mannerisms to vary up my presenting skills?
- Am I talking the whole time or is my team sharing the podium (so to speak)?
- Am I incorporating any element of training?

Note: every meeting should have some element of training. To spice it up a bit, try having one of your senior sales professionals address the group. They won't tune him or her out they same way they tune you out!

Here's another important question to ask yourself: am I ending the meeting in an upbeat fashion? In my last book, *Unleashing your Inner Sales Coach*, I shared my personal favorite method of doing this. I'd like to remind you about Tom, a sales manager I met a few years back. Tom always ends his meetings by saying something nice about his team. He shares a tidbit about great progress in an account or an excellent customer service story. Some weeks, Tom simply tells the team how proud he is or that he's the luckiest manager in the country to have such a talented group.

His words are genuine and appreciative – and those are giant keys with Tom. Speaking of genuine, I remember someone asking me once about the difference between true appreciation and brown-nosing (Which is commonly known as a different phrase that has no place in a book like this!). My answer? Sincerity. The difference between Tom and others is that his words don't come off as patronizing. They are his real feelings and everyone knows it. He's sincere.

The final question is crucial: do our meetings leave my people *better* than before? That is, are they *better* able to sell products than before the meeting started? Are they *better* motivated than before the meeting started? *Better* able to answer customer questions? Yes, better informed, but knowing more about the company's goals, deals and products is only half the battle.

Undoubtedly, you know that meetings take away potentially valuable time that could be spent with customers. So if you're not choosing topics that will help your team do a better job of building brands and serving customers, your people are better off out on the field of play.

Avoiding the weekly data dump is a big part of that. Surely, with all the new methods of communication (email, company portals, etc.), you can find a way to disseminate data effectively. Use that time instead to share ideas and listen to your people. Before you know it, meetings will be viewed in a positive fashion and not just as a date on the calendar to throw darts at.

That's just the way it works.

MISTAKE 13

ENABLING YOUR FRIENDS

Are you able to stand up to your "friends"?

When I say friends, I'm not speaking of Facebook friends or your fishing, golfing, and bowling buddies. I'm talking about the hard-working professionals you used to work alongside of and now manage! It's a type of management that doesn't take place in cyberspace and comes up more than you'd think.

Like when I was talking to Henry recently, who asked me the following question:

"I have an individual, Chad, who I'd like to promote, but I'm worried about his personal relationships with the people he'd likely manage. Should this concern me?"

What do you think? Would you be concerned?

I would! The move from buddy to boss is a difficult transition for many new managers. It's one of the more challenging management situations; as going from a friend to a boss creates a minefield of awkwardness, hurt feelings, and exploitation that can explode at any moment.

But, sometimes, the best candidate is an individual who has deep personal relationships with coworkers and, unfortunately, hiring managers and others who do the promoting don't always have the privilege of being selective.

Sometimes, especially in a pinch, you have to take what you can get.

Managing "friends" is doable but requires some thought early on in the process. Understandably, if and when Chad is installed, he can't simply *"un-friend"* the people he's been *hanging* with for several years.

Henry must understand that Chad is going to have to adjust to a whole different set of professional and social demands. Before promoting, ask Chad if he thinks he'll be able to objectively critique somebody with whom he used to work. More importantly, ask Chad if he can deal *honestly* with a "friend".

To determine the chances for success in a management position, Chad should interview with other top management. He should be put through the paces to isolate behavioral tendencies, in order to shed some light on how he will handle situations involving "friends".

Present him with different scenarios to evaluate his potential reactions.

As an example, consider what the new leadership of the Chicago Cubs did differently as they hired Dale Sveum to be their manager in November 2011. Yes, they waited until November to announce the hire – to keep up their long-standing tradition of *having nothing to do with the World Series*…

Anyway, under the old regime, a typical interview question might have been, *"Where do you see the team in 5 years?"* Or *"What is your philosophy on playing veterans versus younger players?"* Perhaps even *"Do you think the team will still have a chance come Memorial Day?"*

Ok, maybe not that last question but the Cubs' new interview process was quite a bit different from the old method. (Why the change in strategies? I can think of 103 reasons; the number of years since the last championship. You can probably tack on a few more by the time you read this!)

But I digress (again), here's how it was reported in the Chicago Tribune.

"One part of the process is game simulations, in which the candidate is handed lineup cards, statistics, a history of the relievers' workloads, and other relevant facts. A candidate will watch a tape of a game with the Cubs' brass, who will stop the tape at various junctures to ask the candidate what he would do in a particular situation."

As if that wasn't hard enough, they actually threw all the candidates in front of the media to gauge how they handle pressure. Talk about trial by fire!

See what I mean? It was a different process altogether.

So what can you do if you find yourself in this situation?

With a prospective manager, you could highlight situations like a "friend" being late for work or a "friend" failing to execute a critical expectation. Ask the manager what would be done if "friends" tried to take advantage of the "friendship"? Or what to do if the "friend" thought he didn't have to follow protocol because of his special relationship? Create different scenarios, and seek to determine your manager's gut instincts for navigating these waters. Ask the candidate how he or she would respond in a way that maintains a high level of respect but gets the point across. How will he or she stay strong while the "friend" is saying, *"Come on! It's me! Do I really have to do that?"*

It's easy for Chad to say he will handle tricky situations professionally, without letting friendships get in the way. However, if you present a few different scenarios, you might have a higher degree of comfort.

But even *that* might not be good enough for your comfort level, so whatever you do, keep your pulse on the situation, and tell Chad exactly what you expect of him now and in the future.

You'll both be better off.

That's just the way it works.

MISTAKE 14

EXPECTING SUCCESS WITHOUT PROVIDING GUIDANCE

I believe that many managers are *better at setting goals than helping their people reach those goals.* Said differently, many managers expect success without providing the guidance necessary to achieve such success.

I feel this way because I've seen and experienced many situations where managers excel at setting targets but then mistakenly assume that their people have the tools (or possess the smarts) to reach those targets. That's *naïve* – in my book.

And on Fridays, in sales meetings all over the country, irate (and stressed out) managers pound their fists on the proverbial table and demand more sales. But does this brow-beating really help sales professionals create a solid plan for finding those cases?

I'm not so sure.

I *can* tell you that I enjoyed the words I heard from a manager in Nashville recently.

Her company had a renewed focus (goal) on a staple item, and instead of *going nuts* on her team, she simply asked the following:

"What information can I provide to help you achieve this goal?"

Her team responded by asking for lists of:

- Accounts that were currently listed as being out of stock for the product
- Accounts that were currently listed as being out of stock for similar products
- Accounts that had purchased limited quantities of the product in the last 90 days
- Accounts that had purchased similar products in the last 90 days
- Accounts with positive sales trends
- Accounts that were new to the company

- Accounts with operating themes that would benefit by having the product

They simply wanted information that she had access to. After running the reports and giving her team time to review the information, she asked her second *power* question of the day.

"How can we sell more of this product?"

Notice that she didn't say, *"How can you sell more?"* She included herself in the process. Her team took note of her respect and brainstormed before ultimately coming up with an account-by-account strategy for increased selling success. She helped her people develop a strategy that took emotion out of the equation.

By "emotion," I'm referring to selling professionals who pre-judge their customers. In other words, they arbitrarily decide who will and won't be interested in a new offering. It's a slippery slope, to say the least, as it's much easier to find a reason why someone won't be interested than the alternative.

The manager helped her team expand its pool of potential customers.

And they achieved the goal, with her help and the concerted effort of the team.

She was an anomaly. She set the usual *naivety* aside and asked the right questions instead of simply expecting her team to *"go get it done",* and assuming that everything would go smoothly.

As a result, she both helped set the goal *and* guided her team towards achieving the goal.

Do the same, and you'll see similar results because…

That's just the way it works!.

MISTAKE 15

FAILING TO ASK YOUR PEOPLE
HOW YOU CAN SUPPORT THEM

One of the greatest challenges for any manager (especially a new manager) is to lose the "me first" (self-centered) focus and concentrate on the needs of his or her professionals. Not too long ago, I had the opportunity to coach a brand spankin' new team leader, who had just been promoted days before.

I suggested an exercise to do with his team that works well for new managers, experienced managers, and, most importantly, those managers who know deep in their hearts that they should start thinking more of others than themselves.

You know who you are!

As many of you have management experience and have been with your teams for a while, I suggest you try the following exercise sooner rather than later.

Step 1: Say the following:

"I've been remiss in not doing this sooner. What would you think about us getting together for a beer (insert your beverage of choice here) and a brief conversation? The sole purpose of the conversation will be for YOU to tell ME how I can better support YOU. What do YOU think?"

Please consider a couple of important notes:

1) Don't call it a "meeting"! Call it a get-together, a chat, or a conversation. Nobody in his or her right mind wants to attend another meeting.

2) Notice the phrase, "I've been remiss". Saying this or something similar models accountability on your part. If you feel that you've dropped the ball on the substance of this type of conversation, then taking it upon yourself is a great start towards the new you, a leader who is less "me-focused". Choose

whatever words make you most comfortable. Here are some other conversation starters: "I should've done this sooner...", "I've been meaning to do this...", or "I apologize for not asking this question sooner..."

3) Notice that you're not saying, "I need to see you next Tuesday." A big part of the process is respecting your professional, and calling him or her to another mandatory meeting is not the right call. You're asking a collaborative question, and most of your people will respond with a resounding YES, especially if you ask the question in the way I've described above. Actually, just the act of phrasing the request as a question goes a long way towards inclusion, which is the desire of every associate — being included in the process.

4) "Let the silence do the heavy lifting". I read this quote recently in a great book by Author Susan Scott. In short, she uses this phrase to describe the notion of keeping your mouth closed so your conversation partner can (and has time to) respond. It's not easy as many of us are afraid to "let there be silence". Instead of having patience and letting others respond, most jump right in at the first sign of silence. Let's face it. Silence is uncomfortable.

After you ask your initial question about having this chat, make sure to give your associate time to answer, as the words might not come quickly.

Step 2: Choose a time and place.

Assuming you have buy-in on the concept of the "how can I support you" chat, it's time to set a time and place. Say the following:

"What day next week is convenient for you?" And follow that question up with "Where and at what time?"

I like to think this is simple but not easy. Sure, it's simple (in theory) to let your associates win the logistical battle, but it's not easy when you have to shoehorn this "chat" into your busy schedule. Exert too much influence here, and this "chat" becomes just another corporate-mandated meeting in your professional's mind.

The goal is to win the war and not every battle. The war is improved communication with your associates; the battle is choosing which Starbucks (or which out-of-the-way nook) is best to convene at. Showing empathy for the trials and tribulations of your associate's day is a great respect-builder. Meet him or her out on their route for the best results, and if someone goes out of his or her way, let it be you.

Step 3: Once you've set the logistics, say the following:

"So that I may make the most efficient use of YOUR time, please come prepared to discuss 3 ways that I may better support YOU. Please be very specific, and have examples ready to share of areas where I may need to improve. That's what we'll discuss for most of our time together (including anything else you might want to talk about), and at the end (if time permits), I'd like to share 3 ways that you can support me."

You might get the following question: "Am I in trouble?"

If you do, then go back to the beginning. "Not at all! As you may know, I'm trying to improve the ways that I support YOU, and I've been remiss in not asking you this simple question sooner. I'm eager to see what YOU come up with. Thank you, in advance, for taking the exercise seriously."

Please note that you're taking two giant steps forward here with your professional.

1) You're modeling accountability. You could easily say (or think), "This is information that YOU, Mr. or Ms. Professional, should already be sharing with me." But that thought process is counterintuitive. As a manager, you can't demand accountability. That's up to the individual. All you can do is model accountability and create an environment in which your individuals are motivated to do the same.

2) You're also leading by example. Just the simple statement "I'm trying to improve my skills" will go a long way. As you probably know from your own experiences, you can't force someone to improve. Instead, it's better to create the initiative (in his or her mind) to make a few changes. By modeling a more accountable demeanor, there is a much greater chance that your professional will improve if you're doing the same.

It's not fool proof, but it's a step in the right direction!

Please understand that laying the proper foundation is the most important factor for success in any conversation. My take from coaching hundreds of managers is that the little things (like time and place) matter a great deal, and high levels of respect will equate to more acceptance of your coaching efforts.

That's exactly what you want, and that's just the way it works!

·

MISTAKE 16

FOCUSING ON THE WRONG THINGS

"It's somewhere in this room."

That's the reply my wife received at a store in our local mall one afternoon.

Jill saw a blouse she liked on a mannequin, and it must have been really "cute" because she asked for her size.

That's when the sales associate replied, *"It's somewhere in this room."* Then she walked away, leaving us in a room with literally thousands of garments.

I wondered if the blouse was playing a spirited game of hide and seek. I pictured Jill looking through row after row of garments, and the sales associate urging her on by saying, *"Warmer, warmer, cooler, freezing…"*

I wondered if there was a reward being offered for the safe return of a size-2, summer-like blouse?

Well, anyway, Jill did without the "cute" blouse because we couldn't find the right size and the whole experience got me thinking.

What a terrible way to treat your greatest commodity, a ready and willing customer!

Unfortunately, I see this attitude all the time — a gross indifference towards customers. And it's surprising to me because we're coming out of the worst recession in 70 years (any day now), and you'd think retailers would care. Customer demographics and overall economics have really changed. And much to the chagrin of the stores at our local mall, chains like Walmart and Costco are eating these businesses for lunch.

Check out some statistics I recently read about Walmart:

- Walmart had sales in 2010 of $405 billion.
- Walmart has more employees than the U.S. Army.
- Walmart does more business in a day than the GDP of many countries.
- Walmart has 34 million daily customers.

What a juggernaut! The store in the local mall will never beat Walmart on price, especially on brand names. Further, Walmart and others will shine on assortment and logistics, and they certainly can run a tighter ship as far as expenses are concerned.

But specialty stores can win in the areas of customer care and product knowledge.

If they're focusing on the right things.

They can respond to customers like Jill in a way that the bigger stores can't and simply don't care to. They can be excited that customers have chosen their store.

So, what's the remedy? What can a manager do?

Start by continually explaining and reinforcing the importance of a willing and able customer.

Focus on the customer.

When hiring store associates — especially younger ones — instead of spending their training days (or day) showing them how to fold garments and/or ring the register, try the following instead. Share that when a customer walks through the door, he or she has chosen your place of business. Share the reality that your products are no different from what you can find at mass merchandisers. Sure, there are little nuances here and there that serve to separate, but, at the end of the day, everything is pretty much the same. Share that a customer walking through the door is a good thing! A positive occurrence! Not someone who prevents you from putting away stock, taking a break to text your boyfriend or girlfriend, or enjoying a little peace and quiet.

That's the mistake: focusing on the wrong things. Smart managers don't make that mistake.

Instead of boring your new associate with some useless corporate policy about breaks or overtime, etc., focus on the customer. Share that customers who shop in your place of business come for the experience. Share that if they cared only about price, they would buy everything they own at Costco.

And they can't possibly do that.

After all, where would they put it all? You can't buy one hammer at Costco; you have to buy eight hammers.

MC Hammer doesn't even need eight hammers!

No. Your customers don't buy everything at Costco, so when a customer like Jill identifies a *must-have* item, help her find the object of her desire. If you do, then she'll probably come back and buy more.

That's just the way it works. (I'm sure we can find more room in the closet!)

MISTAKE 17

FORGETTING TO APOLOGIZE

My son Danny had his cast removed the other day.

He broke his wrist in a freak bicycle accident. He says his chain came loose. I prefer to think that he was helping an elderly woman cross the street when the accident occurred. My story shows bravery and selflessness.

He doesn't like that story; he'd rather tell the truth. I guess I can't argue with that...

Anyway, the other day at the orthopedist's office, we waited about 90 minutes for an X-ray and a little sawing to remove the cast. I have to admit that the wait grated on me a bit.

Not because I'm impatient, which I am, but because every time we go to this office, we wait at least 60 minutes. Often, we wait longer.

After the cast was safely removed (and after they had moved the saw away from Danny), I mentioned the excessive wait to the doctor.

I was very nice about it. I said, *"We love the care we're receiving here, and we have questions about how long we customarily wait for treatment to begin after our appointment time."*

With this, I recounted our past history of long waits.

To her credit, the doctor was nice and smiled warmly, as she laid out a few excuses. Apparently, a couple of the appointments before ours had been trickier. Both involved upcoming surgeries, and one case involved a special needs child.

She had to spend more time with those families, and I'd want the same treatment if it were my boys.

I understand how that can happen. I was mostly just venting, which is usually all people want to do when they're frustrated.

But she forgot to do one thing. She never said, *"I'm sorry!"*

That's a problem in my book.

When things go wrong (and yes, waiting 60 minutes past your appointment time counts as a thing going wrong), customer service providers must apologize if there is to be any type of closure. (Yes, I consider doctors to be customer service providers!)

Without the apology, the excuses rang hollow, leaving me with two memories: (1) the long wait and (2) the excuses.

When situations with your people (or customers for that matter) don't go as planned, remember to apologize. Don't let ego get in the way. I know Elton John sings, *"Sorry seems to be the hardest word!"* but it doesn't have to be. After all, it's just two words and a few more syllables, a veritable slam-dunk for charades. Say it with me: "I'M SORRY!" See, it's not so hard.

Really, whenever you've made a mistake or find yourself on the wrong side of right, a heartfelt apology will go a long way...

... Towards keeping your people happy.

That's just the way it works.

MISTAKE 18

GIVING UP ON A CUSTOMER

We were about halfway through a sales and service seminar when I spotted a manager named Saul looking like he wanted to ask a question.

By the look on his face, it seemed like I was saying something that didn't sit well with him. Or it could have been the tuna fish. It *was* after lunch.

Anyway, after some cajoling, I got Saul to share what was on his mind.

Here was his question: "I see what you're saying, but I think these strategies work more with a friendly account. What if we're second fiddle in an account? What if the customer is *in bed* with the competitor – so to speak? What do we do in that case?"

Saul's question was a good one; a question that I've heard many time before. What makes this dilemma challenging is that Saul and his sales professionals only have so much time in a day. It's a time management problem, really, but it also poses a question that affects his sales team. How much time does he allocate to accounts owned by the competition, and what message is he sending by suggesting that his people should allocate less time in these accounts?

Well, for purposes of this chapter, I label *giving up* as management mistake. I feel this way because I know how many managers react when faced with this situation. I see many managers give up too easily. It's just simpler to go where it's more comfortable.

We all know that.

But comfort over perseverance teaches your sales professionals an unfortunate lesson: that overcoming difficult situations isn't possible. That being creative won't help. So what do the sales professionals do? They end up fishing where the fish are biting.

Which isn't such a bad idea.

I know it's confusing; let me shed some light on the subject.

I say to keep trying, but only if the playing field is level. In other words, if the competitor isn't playing by the rules, then I suspect it's a better use of your time to focus elsewhere. (See what I mean about time management? So much of smart management boils down to how you use your time! What you choose to do and, more importantly, what you choose not to do.)

So if you determine that the playing field is level, it's time for an honest assessment.

In what ways does your company excel over the competition? What are your strengths and weaknesses? Be real, though. This is not the time to say, "We're good at everything and they suck at life!" That won't get you very far.

How do you compare in the following areas: overall responsiveness, accuracy of information, delivery, customer service, merchandising support, deal structure, ease of doing business, etc?

Are you learning about the decision-maker? What does he or she like about the competitor? Why does his or her company give your competitor the lion's share of business? What are his or her criteria for making decisions? Have these criteria changed recently? If so, how have the criteria changed?

Find out what you can about the sales professional in your competitor's account. What are his or her strengths and weaknesses?

Additionally…

- Don't stress price and price alone. Anyone can deal on price, but that advantage only lasts for so long. Go with creativity. That's a harder *roe to hoe*, but one that leads to sounder financial dealings.

- Don't disparage the competition – if you do, you're implying that your customer has made a bad decision. Also, I know you may have a few little snide remarks about the competitor on the tip of your tongue. It's best to leave those sentiments unsaid. Remember what your mother taught you. *If you don't have anything nice to say…*
  …I shouldn't have to tell you how that one ends.

By disparaging the competition, you're effectively condemning your customer's decision-making process – no matter how flawed it might be. I'm sure we both can think of better strategies than bruising your customer's ego.

- Don't cross over to the dark side – even when the situation seems the darkest. By this expression I mean giving your integrity the day (or week) off. Comprising your values. You know, free merchandise *falling of the truck, sharing your commission* to make the price more appealing, etc. Stay above that nonsense; it's a terribly slippery slope. Once you start giving away the kitchen sink, the house can't be far behind.

- Don't play second fiddle or act like you're a second-class citizen.

On the last bullet above – think of the expression *fake it till you make it*. You'll get a lot further playing the part of the preferred provider rather than taking a back seat.

Do try to cultivate more relationships. Get to know more people. Try to get a sense of how things get done in that business. Educate these customers on the dynamics of a successful business relationship with you and how your company stands out. How you as a service provider stand out from the competition. What you as a service provider bring to the table.

Sometimes, you just have to show these customers how you're able and willing to help them. But whatever you do, please don't make the mistake of giving up easily and sharing that message with your sales professionals.

Keep stressing incremental gains. Keep celebrating small achievements. Keep chipping away and looking for opportunities. All this will help build business and cultivate stronger customer relationships.

Most importantly, though, such skills will help your people deal with adversity in the future. As you well know, not all customers are handed over on a silver platter.

That's just the way it works..

MISTAKE 19

HANDLING ROUTINE PROBLEMS FOR YOUR PEOPLE

When our youngest son Ben turned 9, Jill started to work again. She had been a teacher before her first pregnancy, and recently she started helping out at her dad's optometry practice a couple days a week. (By the way, notice I didn't say our first pregnancy. She was pregnant; I was not. I did put on a few pounds in subsequent years but I assure you I wasn't pregnant even though my children suggested I was.)

Anyway, despite the fact that she works in her father's office, she is vehement about not using her cell phone while working, and that's a bit of a problem for me. See, when I'm in town, I'm used to reaching her whenever I need her. Often, it's just to say hello or something similarly trivial, but other times, it's to ask a question about the boys.

Can they have this for lunch? Can they go here? Should I make them do their homework? How do you make a scrambled egg? Where's the Neosporin?

It's stupid stuff, really, but I'm used to being able to get her on the line. I've relied on her for a long time, and, as a result, I haven't been making routine decisions (or handling the simple tasks) that I'm fully capable of handling. (I think.)

Can you people handle simple tasks? (Be honest...)

The reason I ask is that I see the same dynamic play out every day between managers and sales professionals.

Here's what I mean. Often, when I coach, a manager will say, "I have an individual who calls me off the hook 10 to 15 times a day, and I don't know how to stop it. They ask me questions that I know they're capable of answering on their own. What do I do?"

They're usually pretty frustrated!

Here's my take: You know the expression, "You get what you tolerate"? This manager is getting repeated phone calls because he tolerates repeated phone calls.

Does this sound like you? Try the following:

Set a daily call-in time for your sales professional. In other words, except for emergencies, have him or her call you once a day to go over open items, questions, concerns, etc.

If you have sales professionals who are particularly needy, start with two calls a day.

Among the many advantages, I can see one distinct benefit for both of you.

For you, there will be fewer interruptions and more productivity.

For the sales professional, he or she will begin building the skills necessary to handle routine obstacles and solve problems without your help. And that's a big deal for his or her development.

Let me warn you. At first, your people won't see it that way. They're probably used to having you as a security blanket. You'll have to sell this concept by pointing out the advantages **for the sales professional**. In a fit of desperation, I've heard of many managers communicate the need for a set call-in time so they (the manager) aren't interrupted as much.

That's not the right strategy because that sentiment is about the manager, instead of being more geared towards the sales professional. In my estimation, most sales professionals want the answer when they want the answer. Sometimes, they truly need the answer, at a moments notice, but other times it's not so urgent. It's the latter category where, if sales professionals learn to collect their thoughts and questions, then they will deviate from their daily plan less frequently. Ultimately, allowing your people to handle their own routine problems will lead to more productivity and, in time, more sales. All desirable goals for the sales professional.

Managers just have to help their people see it that way.

So, I'm not going to call Jill about Ben's sunscreen. I'm going with the SPF 100.

Good luck, sun!

Why such a high SPF? Have you seen me? I look like I've lived my whole life in a basement. Unfortunately for Ben, the apple doesn't fall far from the tree!

Much like I can decide what type of sun block to put on Ben, your people can handle the little issues that crop up during the day. But they're never going to develop problem-solving skills if you don't afford them that opportunity.

That's just the way it works.

.

.

MISTAKE 20

HEARING, BUT NOT LISTENING

Do you ever watch those incredible music award shows? You know, the ones where all the stars strut their stuff on the big stage in outrageous costumes?

Last November, we recorded the American Music Awards, and the other day, I was watching the Black Eyed Peas perform their hit song *It's going to be a great day*. What an amazing act. They're quite the performers, but I have to tell you that the combination of lights, action, singing, and dancing is a bit over stimulating.

With all the visual stimulation and the group's outlandish full-body armor drawing my attention, it's hard to actually concentrate on the music.

Reminds me of life today.

I think we all suffer from *collective ADD*.

Why? Well, each day, we're bombarded with so much useless information, and our minds are constantly cluttered. Life today consumes so much energy, and often, when we try to communicate with someone, our words are lost in the midst of all the distractions. As a defense mechanism, we leave our homes wearing our own versions of the Black Eyed Peas' *full-body armor* to protect ourselves. We're hesitant to let others in because we can't separate the "noise" from those who'll really listen to us. In some ways, it's like we don't know who to trust.

And managers who hear us, but don't really listen to what we're saying, compound our feelings.

Hearing is one thing, but listening is quite another.

Having people feel that you're truly listening to them these days is difficult, but not insurmountable, and it's one of the greatest skills of leadership.

Here are a few thoughts so that you can *help people feel heard*.

You help others feel heard by turning down the volume of your ego and turning up the volume of your listening. You do this by not always having to be the one with the right answer.

You help others feel heard by being the *one* person who makes them feel that you're sincerely listening and that the world around them has stopped for a moment. You know how good that feels.

You help others feel heard by putting down your mobile device and distancing yourself from all distractions, thereby giving your people a gift most have never received — your full attention!

This, after all, is one of the premises upon which this book is written. That's how important it is.

You help others feel heard by asking clarifying questions. Some examples are:

- *What does that mean?*
- *Can you be more specific?*
- *How did you reach that conclusion?*
- *Can you share some examples?*
- *What do you really mean?*
- *Can you clarify that for me?*
- *What are the implications of that statement?*

There are many other options for effective clarifying questions. The key is to ask something that (1) gets you more information and (2) shows that you're listening.

And what happens if you fail to listen? Great question. I hear you loud and clear on that one! Well, you'll certainly fail to learn what's important to others, and they may stop communicating with you. Most importantly, though, if you listen, you may hear what *isn't* being said. Reminds me of the old Cherokee saying, *"Listen to the whispers, and you won't have to hear the shouts."*

Isn't the Internet great? (How else would I know what the Cherokees are saying?)

You help others feel heard by not interrupting, by letting them finish their sentences.

You help others feel heard by concentrating on what they are saying, not what you're going to say. A common detriment to poor listening is not letting someone complete his or her thought. For example, a colleague may be asking a two-part question; however, because you're formulating your answer to the first part, you don't hear the second part. Your colleague must then repeat the question, which wastes their time and shows a lack of respect.

So, if you want your people to take off their protective armor and share with you, you'll have to focus, reconnect, and satisfy their hunger to be heard You'll have to truly listen. And if they feel heard, *it's going to be a great day!*

That's just the way it works!

MISTAKE 21

IGNORING RECESSION-ERA ECONOMICS

One of my favorite pastimes is teaching retail wine associates the intricacies of suggestion selling. I always start with the following premise: if a customer wants to spend $10, with the right amount of knowledge and training, any wine associate should be able to sell a $12 bottle.

That seemingly measly $2 difference is a greater benefit than meets the eye. After all, that's extra money falling right to the bottom line. Those extra dollars can add up in a hurry. A few extra dollars matters more than it would appear, especially in the midst of the never-ending great recession.

But not all managers explain it that way.

Not long ago, I was teaching a group of wine professionals and a young lady shared the following: "The bottom-liners may not like this, but if the customers asks for a $10 bottle, I have to give a $10 bottle to keep my credibility!"

The bottom-liners?

My initial thought was quite simple. "Wait, what? The owners?"

The finance people? You mean the people with the responsibility of keeping the ship afloat? The bean counters, if you will?

You could cut the ideology with a knife. Make that a chain saw!

I immediately wondered about her manager. What type of message was her manager sending about up-selling and suggestion selling? Did the wine sales associate understand that when you up-sell, not only are you providing a service, but also bringing in extra revenue that benefits the company immensely? Was the manager communicating any of that?

My guess is no.

To be sure, you never steer a customer from what he or she has asked for, ever! If the customer comes in asking for the Chateau Purple Forest, then that's what you give the customer. Further, you always sell quality. Dumping bad wine on unsuspecting and/or naïve people is an unwise practice at best.

Talk about losing credibility!

But in the wine business (as in any business), if the customer asks for a recommendation, your job is to steer the customer towards the best bottle in that price range. That's your job as the expert – and it's a great way to add value. Sure, some customers have a firm budget and will balk at anything over their stated limit, but others will spend a few extra dollars if given good reason.

That's where the selling comes in and where you have to provide a good reason to buy.

I would say the following: "There are many great selections in the $10 range and I have this excellent selection at $12. The Green Apple Chardonnay is wonderful for these reasons. It's delicious and versatile. The wine has antioxidants and is one of our best organic selections. It pairs well with most everything. Yes, it's a few bucks more but definitely worth it."

Then you could say, "Would you like to try a bottle?"

Take a shot! You're not suggesting Mouton, for crying out loud. (As you may know, Mouton Rothschild retails from $200 to $2,000 dollars a bottle or more. This is a bit harder to sell – and even harder to find someone willing to share some with me.)

The key is to have a sense of the price ranges and styles customers routinely ask for. This way you'll be ready. I suggest keeping a log for a few weeks of exactly the kinds of requests you get. If $10 reds are asked for most of the time, than you have no reason to not be prepared to up-sell a customer who comes in asking for a $10 red.

One caveat, though, speaking of credibility: if the customer is adamant about his or her preferred price range, then you owe it to the customer to back off. Becoming a pushy sales person is not the goal!

Actually, the "bottom-liners" comment took me back several years to my independent retail days. Many years ago, I think it was more acceptable to find the perfect bottle of wine for your customers. If the customer was preparing her favorite *duck a l'orange* recipe, you gave her a wine that brought out the flavors perfectly. Price and margin were important, but not as much as today. Nowadays, if your customer is preparing her favorite duck recipe, your goal is still, of course, to select a wine that brings out the flavors perfectly. But now, it's also imperative to bring out those amazing flavors with a selection that's important to the company.

Ideology has been replaced by other words that end in "y", like solvency and liquidity. And managers must communicate that so wine associates can balance their desire to choose the perfect product (and build their credibility) with the company's need for profitability. Yep, another word that ends in a "y".

And if you're out there selling wine to consumers, given the prolonged economic slump, you really have no choice but to try to dig as deep as you can into your customers' pockets.

It's imperative for managers to teach this concept. Sometimes customers *don't know what they don't know*, you know? A slightly higher-priced bottle may complete their meal better; make their occasion just a bit more special. So we teach them, and in the process we earn a few extra dollars.

It's a perfect example of a win-win situation. The customers win, and so do the bottom-liners.

After all, got to keep the bottom-liners happy.

That's just the way it works.

MISTAKE 22

LETTING TIME CONTROL YOU

I didn't go there for a medal or for the thrill of victory. I simply wanted to run a local race with some friends. So one warm Sunday morning, we all toed the line at the Deerfield Dash 5K and 10K. It was a recreational crowd, to say the least. A few runners had steaming cups of Latte. Caffeinated, of course. A guy in an Elvis costume. Lots of children, people running with dogs, and so on.

You get the picture. There weren't too many serious runners.

The race started and, after a few hundred yards, I realized that I was in first place; a position completely new to the likes of me. I did come in second place once in a high school race, but I never tasted victory. Yes, there were people behind me that day – and I resent you asking that question.

Anyway, there I was in the lead, running right behind the police car. Could this be the day? Could I be destined for Deerfield Dash greatness? Was I going to be forever immortalized in the winner's circle – someone the locals would talk about for years to come? Would I be on the cover of the Deerfield Review? Would my finisher's photo be tweeted (and re-tweeted) by running enthusiasts all over the world? Would I have something *marginally* interesting to post on my Facebook page? Would my story go viral? A story of success, despite overwhelming obstacles, that others could learn from? Did the Deerfield Dash have a course record?

Have I built enough suspense? Ok, I'll get on with the story already.

After a mile or so, the police car continued on the 10K route and I continued the 5K all by my lonesome. There were no other runners in sight.

That's when the trouble started.

I reached the proverbial fork in the road; a four-way intersection with no signs. I felt like Dorothy on the yellow brick road, except I didn't have a scarecrow to tell me which way to go.

Sadly, I don't think the wizard could have helped me that day.

And yes, you guessed it: I went the wrong way. When I reached the pivotal point, instead of going straight, I turned, despite there not being any signs telling me to do so.

Talk about being a *weenie*!

I'll tell you how the race ended at the end of this chapter. Suffice it to say, I wish I'd looked at a course map that morning, as that would have helped me know where to go.

There would have been a better outcome than almost ending up in a different area code.

So my question to you is, do you have a course map for the busy race known as your day? When you get to the critical intersection of your day, do you know which way to go? Are you running ragged without a clue how to get to the finish line? Are you controlling time or is time controlling you?

Ask the following questions and you'll be much more likely to stay on course with your plans and your day!

Are you starting the day with a brief planning session?

This is the most important question of all. The strongest piece of advice I can give any professional is to start each day with some time for planning. Too many individuals jump right to the first task, which isn't always the activity with the most importance. It's relatively simple! While sipping your caramel macchiato, spend some time contemplating what would make this day successful. Gauge your preparedness for the day. Anticipate (and try to handle proactively) any risks that might knock you off your plan.

Are you writing out your daily objectives?

Mental notes are vague and ill defined. Writing your objectives pulls your energy to the target. I've seen so many examples of success just by virtue of a manager taking the time to put this structure around his objectives.

Are you sticking to your plan?

How do you handle interruptions? It's always good to ask, "Is what I'm about to do more important than what I planned to do?" Ask this question anytime something random and unexpected threatens to knock you off your plan.

Are you writing everything down?

Writing everything down clears the head and allows for more creativity. Just this act alone also increases the likelihood that you will follow through. Writing everything down also reduces the chance of important items falling through the cracks.

Do you review your notes, plans and objectives as the day goes on?

Your situation (and your reality) is constantly changing. Plus, it's mentally nourishing to see what you've accomplished. It gives you a little boost as the day progresses.

Are you handling your most important priorities first?

In the morning, you're at your best. It's easier to resist interruptions and, if nothing else, when you handle your most important items first, at least you will have accomplished your most important task if the day spirals out of control. (Which it probably will!)

Are you preparing for the defining moment?

The defining moment is the period of time during which the critical ingredients of success are present. This is the time when thinking and advance preparation come in handy. Spend some time anticipating roadblocks, objections and other obstacles and prepare a plan for handling these defining moments in a proactive manner.

Are you effectively dealing with frustration?

Frustration and the resulting inability to take action is a huge time-waster. A good practice is to stop and evaluate frustrating situations. Actually pause and take a good look at what's happening. Think of positives and visualize the last time you were frustrated. What happened? It likely passed and everything worked out. Right?

Is it okay to allow for some negative time? Sure, you can vent, but only for a short time. If the mood drags on, your day will be forever altered. Take control of the situation. Make sure to ask, "What part of this failure to execute has my name on it?" Take some accountability for the situation, as that will help you move forward.

Are you recapping the day?

Look at your calendar at the end of the day. Did the day go as planned? Was what happened what you wanted to happen? I'm sure a few fires popped up, but did you accomplish your most urgent and important tasks?

Review and document whom you interacted with and whom you need to follow up with. Now is the time to start thinking and noting what needs to happen and whom you need to contact for tomorrow to be a successful day

As I wrote this chapter, I was reminded of something I read in Steve Jobs' biography. Apparently, Jobs had something his co-workers referred to as a *reality distortion field*. Steve was able to "convince himself and others to believe almost anything with a mix of charm, charisma, bravado, hyperbole, marketing, appeasement, and persistence. The *reality distortion field* was said to distort an audience's sense of proportion and scales of difficulties and made them believe that the task at hand was possible."

His ability to see what others couldn't see (or didn't want to see), was a big factor in his success.

He had the privilege of living in this *other world*.

Most of us don't have that luck! Your *reality distortion field* may tell you that you can get everything done, but you can't and you won't. That's why it's so important to plan, adjust and evaluate as the day goes on.

So, as I promised – here's how the Deerfield Dash ended up. After a few minutes of running the wrong way, I got a sinking feeling that something was terribly amiss. I finally re-joined the course in time to come in 3rd place. I can't remember who won, but I do remember who came in second place - a man pushing a twin baby jogger! Ouch! Cute kids, though…

You'd have thought the diaper bag would have slowed him down a little.

My friend who was observing, and wouldn't have lasted past the quarter mile mark, looked at me and said, "What the heck happened to you?" (Except he used more colorful language.)

I'm just glad Runner's World wasn't covering the race! That would've been really embarrassing…

Well, anyway, I wish I had looked at the course map. Glory would have been mine.

And it can be yours as well. As you look at your daily plan, please realize that you're not going to get everything done. The most successful managers and leaders understand that. So they plan relentlessly to allocate, analyze, review and re-view their activities so they can be as efficient as possible. In the end, these individuals still leave for the day with piles on their desks and most likely fall short of accomplishing everything they wanted to.

But they accomplish more done than the "just winging it" crowd. And that's a good thing because you can use every advantage these days.

That's just the way it works.

MISTAKE 23

LOOKING IN THE IMAGINARY MIRROR

Just to be very clear, I don't have an anecdote for this chapter. The reason is because I want the questions and comments to be crystal clear and I don't know how to say the following any more clearly. So I'll just say it.

I find that one of the biggest reasons your associates don't do what you expect them to do is because you as a manager are probably **not clear enough**.

Okay, I said it. And now I'm going to help you.

Here are some questions that will help determine whether you need to make changes in your communication style. The end goal is for your people to do what you ask them to do and when you ask them to do it!

I guess my first question is – **do you have an imaginary mirror?**

The reason I ask is because I can't help but notice that many stories involving a lack of execution come back to the manager not being clear enough. Not all of the time, but enough to make a difference.

I find that many managers look through an imaginary mirror; like the one in Snow White. You remember Snow White – don't you? By virtue of not having any daughters, I actually had to Google Snow White to refresh my memory.

Do you remember how the Queen would address the mirror and say, "Mirror, mirror on the wall, who is the fairest of them all?" And the mirror would respond, "You are, my Queen!" Which, of course, was the answer the queen so desperately wanted to hear.

I had my version of an imaginary mirror when I ballooned up in weight a few years back. I had always been a runner and managed to keep the pounds off, despite a less-than-spectacular diet. Although the reflection in the mirror was larger, I conned myself into thinking I was still my svelte self. I wasn't. One day, I got on my talking scale and it said, "Come back when you're alone…" Ouch!

Had the scale actually said that, it would have been a whole lot more honest than I was. And it would have been quite the scale. Talk about high-tech! And sarcastic…

Anyway, I let my mirror tell me what I wanted to hear.

And I have to ask - do you have an imaginary mirror, like the Queen and I? Does your mirror tell you exactly what you want to hear? Are you fooling yourself or do you allow the answer to be something you can learn from?

The questions that follow are more procedural while the ones we asked above are more about your desire to improve and learn from your actions. Handle the mirror questions with honesty and you'll be well on your way to eliminating this mistake from your repertoire.

Are you going too fast?

Much of the difficulty in successfully conveying your wishes stems from rushing. It's a bit too much of the "hurry up and wait" scenario. Instead, take your time for better results. Just slowing down your rate of speech will help. By the way, being grossly over-distracted and looking the part as well will only serve to create more anxiety for your people. Take a deep breath. If you're more composed, they will be too.

Are you clear enough in your own mind about what you want to convey?

Are you taking the time to clearly and succinctly develop your thoughts? If you asked me that question years ago, I would've answered – NO! Back then, as I'd delegate projects to my team, I'd often conceive an idea and be off to the races. Because I hadn't fully developed the idea in my own mind, there was really no hope of sharing my expectations in a clear, straightforward manner. Speaking of which…

Do you share your expectations in a clear, straightforward manner?

Be succinct and concise. I know, I know. It's easier said than done! Mark Twain pointed this out when he was famously quoted as saying, "I'd have written less if I had more time!" Yes, it takes more time to be concise, and eliminating unnecessary words and verbiage goes a long way. Social media sites like Twitter actually help you curtail your messages but since you don't (I hope) actively tweet your people to hand out assignments, you'll have to find other ways to be clearer.

My suggestion: share what you want to share and then ask for interpretation. Say, "does this make sense?" Or, "sometimes I don't even understand what I'm saying! Am I expressing myself in a clear, straightforward manner?" Remember: it doesn't matter if you think it's clear, it's what the other person thinks.

Do you create a sense of urgency for everything?

Sure, any manager can have an emergency that trumps all the other emergencies. But when every last assignment is handled like civilization is ending, your professionals will have a hard time prioritizing your emergencies. Smart managers use urgency more sparingly. The play the urgency card when it's actually, well, urgent. This way people actually pay attention.

I love the following from an article titled – *10 Things Only Bad Managers Say.* After dropping a dozen equally critical priorities on a professional's desk, if he has read this article, don't be surprised if he says, "Yes, of course. That'll push yesterday's drop-everything project to next Thursday. Is that ok?"

Do you share the *why*?

Do you want people who process tasks with their hearts and minds or with their hands and feet? Trust me: you want the former. To gain the buy-in from your team, share why you are asking your professionals to do said task. How does it fit into the big picture? How does it help the team (and the company) reach its long-term goals? I'm not saying you have to go all Knute Rockne on everyone. As you know, Rockne was the legendary Notre Dame football coach who was known for inspiring with the football team with his legendary speeches.

Inspiring the team to *"win one for the Gipper,"* for every little task is a bit much, but don't do the opposite, either.

Are you helping specify next steps?

Ask - what will you do first to accomplish this task? How will you get started? Specifying the initial step helps, especially if the project consists of a series of smaller steps.

I remember a sales manager telling me how he feels understood as he assigns projects, but not so much afterwards. He notices that, as his people file out of his office, he doesn't get the sense that anyone knows what to do next. He gets a ton of blank, quizzical looks. Make sure to specify next steps and, while you're at it, ask when it would be convenient to check in to ascertain progress. Asking at frequent, unplanned intervals is intrusive and off-putting. Asking when it was agreed that you would ask is keeping up your end of the bargain.

So let me be perfectly clear - taking stock of how you communicate expectations will help create an environment where your people do exactly what you need them to do – when you need them to do it.

That's just the way it works.

MISTAKE 24

"LOSING IT" WITH YOUR PEOPLE

A company executive asked me the following question during a seminar.

Is it ok to "lose it" with my team once in a while?

My reply: "Depends on what you mean by losing it!" Does that mean yelling or merely getting emotional to help underscore an important point?

I've seen people really lose it before. While a college student, I watched legendary Indiana University basketball coach Bobby Knight "lose it" in a major way. He threw a chair clear across the court before he was asked to watch the rest of the game from the locker room.

So my short answer is "Yes!" You can let loose, but how you do so makes a huge difference.

The longer answer is a bit more complicated.

One of my tenets of management is that anything that can be said in a negative manner can also be said in a positive manner. Of course, it takes a bit more effort to say something positively (which is why there is so much negativity in the workplace), but it's inherently possible. When I share this philosophy with managers, inevitably, one will ask, "How do I show that I'm serious or that I'm pissed off?" It's a good question with a somewhat complicated answer.

Let me say first that I'm opposed to negativity in the workplace. I believe that negativity rarely helps, and negative reinforcement doesn't change behavior. Sadly, at one of my clients, the lowest performer is pointed out at every sales meeting. This behavior causes the sales professional to feel worse, not better. And it doesn't improve his performance. Not by a long shot. It actually decreases his level of motivation, though I don't think that's what they're intending to do when they engage in this activity.

To understand this subject further, let's examine the differences between the following statements:

1)   "You guys are killing me! What will it take to get you to execute? I won't listen to another angry supplier because of you guys!"

2)   "I know you guys are better than this. What do **we** have to do differently to execute at the level that I know we're capable of? What is one thing that each of you can do differently to get more placements, etc?"

There are numerous problems with statement #1 and I would categorize it as "losing it!" Not only is it demeaning, but it also puts all the responsibility for improvement squarely on the sales professionals. This statement is also physiologically counterproductive.

To explain, it helps to understand a feeling commonly known as the "runner's high". The runner's high is a term used for the euphoric state experienced by runners during a long run. It's a positive chemical reaction in the brain and the main reason many runners claim they can think more clearly while running.

Yelling at the team or another similarly negative act produces the exact opposite reaction. Many managers let loose on their people and then immediately demand creativity and problem-solving skills. Unlike the runner's high, after such negative reinforcement, the brain isn't able (at that moment) to think clearly and creatively. It's just not possible, and I'm sure you see that by the way people withdraw after a tongue-lashing. The acts of yelling and negativity reduce (eliminate) the good chemicals, and it usually takes at least an hour or more, according to my experience, for any possibility of creativity to be sparked. After that much time has elapsed, everyone has usually gone on his or her merry way. It's too late at that point.

Further, saying "I won't listen to another angry supplier because of you guys!" is clearly a me-centered, egotistical statement. I try to convey this to every company executive. Most of the individuals on the team don't care if the company executive takes a beating.

They care about themselves – which is their right.

Statements directed from the perspective of the individual are much more effective.

Statement #2 involves the manager in the process by saying, "What do we have to do?" This sentiment also pays a compliment and sets up a more conducive environment for problem-solving and creativity. Challenging an individual to make one change is a manageable, bite-size goal that helps, rather than hinders, the process.

One last question: Is it advisable to raise your voice?

Not really. Yelling and being emotional are two different animals. Yelling is just a way for a leader to blow off steam, another egotistical gesture. It's more deflating, not more motivating, and shows a tremendous lack of respect. If you're not sure just take a look at someone's face after you've read him or her the riot act. It's not a pretty picture.

Emotion, on the other hand, is good. Not always, but in selected intervals it's useful to highlight importance and create a sense of urgency. Like anything else, emotion should be a tool in the manager's tool kit. Too much isn't necessarily a good thing. Using emotion properly will allow for an atmosphere that encourages your people to participate in a productive conversation about improvement, accountability, and execution.

In summary, I believe it's ok to "lose it" once in a while as long as yelling and negativity are removed from the equation. That's the line of demarcation in my book.

So go ahead and inspire the troops! Get emotional! Create a sense of urgency and performance will improve.

And you'll likely get fewer calls from angry suppliers!

That's just the way it works!

MISTAKE 25

MISREPRESENTING YOUR COACHING ABILITIES

Often, my managers and I talk about setting priorities and what types of tasks and activities constitute a priority. I remember one conversation in particular. Sam was having trouble finding time to properly coach the members of his team.

I shared with Sam that the question isn't "Can you afford to spend time coaching your people?" Rather, it's "Can you afford not to?"

To start the conversation, I asked Sam, "Do you coach your sales professionals?"

"Of course I do," was his quick reply.

I asked, "So, do you sit down with a clear agenda to talk about issues, opportunities, customers, products, selling situations, motivational strategies, and goals on a weekly or bi-weekly basis?"

"Well, not exactly…"

"Who does most of the talking? You or the sales professional?" I asked.

[Pause...]

(I usually try to let the silence do the heavy-lifting, but Sam needed a little help!)

"Do you collaborate on solutions and then hold your people accountable for a series of actions or steps as a result of your time together?" I asked.

[A slightly longer pause...]

"Do you give out a lot of advice?" I asked.

[The longest pause yet...]

I think you get the picture. Sam, like most managers, thinks he's "coaching," but he's mostly just dispensing advice or "that-a boy" motivational phrases. He's misrepresenting his coaching abilities because he's not really coaching. He's advising.

The problem with advice is twofold. First, it makes a sales professional more dependent on the manager, and second, it's far less likely to be acted upon than your sales professional's ideas for improvement. In reality, his or her idea, although it may be less appealing than yours, will have a much greater likelihood of being acted upon.

I also shared that most sales professionals seek better coaching, or at least coaching of some sort, and the pity is that managers let obstacles (like being too busy) get in the way of providing such development. Even though they place great importance on time spent in coaching and see it as a priority, when push comes to shove, many managers don't allocate enough time — or any time at all. And then they make an excuse or two.

- "I'm too busy."
- "They're too busy."
- "There is no convenient place to meet."
- "Another meeting or event will take precedence."

Please don't misunderstand. I'm not implying that managers aren't busy. I know they are. I see it every time I visit a client. What I am saying is that many managers can improve the way they match their priorities to their activities, because at this point, I sense a great disconnect.

Managers see performance coaching as important, but they don't do it. There are too many fires to put out, too many distractions.

To all managers, I share the same thought. Schedule coaching as you would any other important activity. Put it on the calendar. Book it and do it. Sure, your schedule may get altered. So be it. Reschedule, and move on. Excuses, quite often, are valid and genuine obstacles that you must reckon with and the problem isn't when you recognize such obstacles. The problem occurs when you rely on such excuses, which, in turn, causes a paralyzing lack of activity.

It's when the threat of a meeting or any scheduling difficulty robs a sales professional of a few interrupted minutes to talk strategy or anything else on his or her mind.

That's when you've passed the point of no return.

That's what I see the most and what disturbs me about this dynamic. I know from hundreds of conversations that sales professionals want consistent coaching, and their managers know it.

There's another part of this equation, and this part applies more to those individuals running sales organizations.

Unless you make associate development and coaching part of your manager's evaluation criteria (read: compensation), you probably won't get the type of ongoing development you desire within your company.

It simply won't get done in a manner that benefits your people.

On the other hand, let's say you agree with me and tie coaching and development to your manager's evaluation process. The next question is "How do you know that these conversations are actually taking place in a productive manner?"

You really don't unless you build some accountability into the process.

As an example, here's what I suggest based upon a sales team consisting of 5 sales professionals. These numbers are only meant as a guide. All situations aren't created equally.

I suggest 8 one-on-one conversations a month, along with 2 team meetings.

Have your managers assign the coaching slots based upon experience, need, present situation, or any other relevant factors. Spend more time with the newbies, but don't neglect the top performers or "mature" team members.

After each coaching session, team leaders should fill out a very short recap form with brief answers to the following prompts:

- Who they met with.
- When they met.
- Where they met.
- What customers, products, and/or issues they discussed.
- What action steps (and corresponding timeline) was decided upon.
- How and when they (the manager) will check-in and monitor progress.

This is the accountability part. Without this brief recap, a top-level manager won't be sure that coaching is happening in a productive manner. Additionally, just knowing what your people are talking about will give you more credibility with your sales team.

Yes, a sales manager's responsibilities involve analyzing top line numbers and goals, but having a greater understanding of how your people are moving towards goals (i.e., what new approaches they're trying) is a plus. Knowing this will also give you opportunities to praise your sales professionals for their hard work and improvement.

Hold to the 8 coaching conversations per month. Don't let the busy season get in the way. In other words, if you sell beer, then the crazy summer selling season isn't the time to cut out coaching conversations. This is exactly the time of year when more opportunities are present, and good coaching will help harvest such opportunities.

Don't forget to have people document their action steps, as clearly defined, specific action steps are the main goal with coaching. Without firm action steps for moving forward, coaching is vague and uncertain. Determining next steps and monitoring progress adds certainty to the process and makes outcomes more reachable.

Don't make the mistake of doing the unimportant, and forsaking what is truly important, one-to-one coaching and development.

And remember, the question isn't "Can you afford to spend time coaching?" No. The better question is "Can you afford not to?"

That's just the way it works

MISTAKE 26

NEGLECTING YOUR TOP PERFORMERS

Try the following exercise the next time you have a few minutes.

Take out a sheet of paper, and list the members of your team. Look at the list for a moment, and put one of the following letters by each name: (T) for top performers, (M) for middle performers, and (B) for bottom performers. Choose only one member of your team for the "top performer" designation.

Now, lock your eyes in on the name of your top performer.

I'd like to ask you a few questions.

Do you overlook this individual? Do you take this individual for granted? When is the last time you spent a substantive amount of time with this person? When did you last surprise this individual with a random act of kindness? Have you ever offered to handle his or her duties for an afternoon?

Now, just for kicks, imagine the top performer working across town for your competitor.

How does that feel?

Now, imagine your next vacation…

Wait, will there be a next vacation, or will you be doing his or her work that week if he or she leaves, instead of lying on a beach in Mexico? Because of your need to stay close, will your next vacation be at the local retention pond. A *staycation* – if you will!

Ok, enough of that. Let's put a name behind this nightmare.

Earlier in 2010, I met Hank at a beverage distributor. For three years running, Hank had his team's best numbers, despite having just an average territory. But he felt neglected. He felt that he was taken for granted and couldn't remember the last time his manager worked alongside him or recognized him in any way.

These feelings affected his performance. I'm not saying he dogged it, but he felt he could do more.

Top performers have to be coached just like everyone else. Top performers need to be recognized and acknowledged just like everyone else.

Don't take them for granted. Ask your top performer how he or she likes to be appreciated. Know that appreciation must be valuable to the recipient to have impact. Not all associates like to be acknowledged in the same manner, as some managers would lead you to believe. Don't fall into the trap of thinking that the extra dollars a top performer earns, will negate the need for the appreciation that should come along with it.

As a side note, I routinely survey sales professionals to understand the role of money in motivation. To be sure, a few extra dollars helps but it doesn't sway performance as much as one might think. To gain perspective, I would ask the following question.

What is the best way to motivate you?

The results might surprise you. My analysis shows that only 18% of the answers relate to earning more money. Truthfully, I think that number is a bit too low. Maybe, respondents aren't as forthcoming as I'd like; however, one fact is clear to me.

Money isn't the only motivator. It's a motivator, to be sure; but often not the most important one. A great step is to ask your people the best way to motivate them.

As you accumulate this useful information about your team, watch for signs of discouragement and burnout. Watch for signs that your performers (top or bottom) look overwhelmed. Resist the notion that you're too busy to show appreciation or that your people are too busy to receive it. If you feel overwhelmed, then start making an extra effort with one person. If you feel discomfort in showing appreciation, get over it. It's too important, and the tragedy of neglect is so avoidable. Don't let unrealistic expectations get in the way.

Recently, I read *The Manager's Coaching Handbook* by David Cotrell. Here are a few suggestions for working with top performers based (in part) on this book:

- Get top performers involved in as many decisions as possible.
- Delegate a few projects so top performers feel valued.
- Celebrate their successes much like you would the triumphs of your middle or bottom performers.
- Spend time with top performers (i.e., one-on-one coaching, ride-withs, etc.).
- Listen to the ideas of top performers.
- Help top performers create mentoring-type relationships with their teammates.

One suggestion I always share is to ask top performers to help train the rest of the team. Include an element of peer-to-peer training. That is, let the team hear from someone besides the individuals they typically hear from.

Peer-to-peer training is a wonderful way to share other opinions and make top performers feel valued.

Leave top performers better than before. Unfortunately, it's not the bottom-dwellers who leave on their own to find opportunity elsewhere. Instead, it's the people whose help you need so you can take a vacation once in a while. Don't neglect the top performers, or any performers for that matter. If everyone feels appreciated, your results will be better.

Your *staycations* will turn into vacations – and you'll enjoy them a great deal more.

That's just the way it works!

MISTAKE 27

OVERLOOKING THE 5 P'S OF SUCCESS

"I had a great day today, Dad!"

That's what he said, but I already knew.

On Josh's sixteenth birthday, he had two goals: first, pass his driver's test; second, fly an aircraft for the first time all by his lonesome. To "solo," as the pilots call it.

After he drove himself to the airport, he calmly piloted a Sportstar (N912PV) aircraft down the runway and up into the sky.

It was truly a sight to see. But that's not the whole story and certainly not the main reason for sharing this with you.

How Josh accomplished his dream of piloting N912PV is a great lesson for us all. It highlights several important lessons with great parallels for success in your life and the lives of your associates.

It also counts as a management mistake in my book.

Too many managers ignore these lessons: **P**ractice, **P**erseverance, **P**reparation, **P**riority, and **P**assion.

I call them the "5 Ps" of piloting (or success).

Let's examine each trait individually, along with some questions that (1) your associates should be asking of themselves and (2) that you should be asking of them.

First, Josh **practiced** religiously for his special day. There were some days when he and his flight instructor, Ted, landed the Sportstar 15 or more times in one single lesson. That's also 15 takeoffs for those of you keeping track at home. (Never mind! You can't land if you don't take off!) Why does that amuse me???

Anyway, Josh and his instructor practiced every type of flight situation. Stalls, landing with crosswinds, flying in another plane's wake, etc. Push the nose up, push it down. Bank left, bank right. All kinds of maneuvers. Before last Thursday, Josh had practiced most every situation that might occur while he was flying.

How much are your people practicing? Are they ready for the inevitable moment of truth that happens in every sales call? Can they handle all that might come their way? Do they practice saying their most important points out loud before a critical call? Sure, it's cliché, but practice certainly does make perfect. Good practice, that is!

Do your associates practice selling the new craft beer to their fellow sales professionals? To their manager? I know nobody likes to be dragged up in front of the room for role-playing, but what about practicing how to sell the hot new beer or wine in a quiet office? It's not the same as a customer call, to be sure, but if they pay attention, then they'll get a sense as to whether they have their facts straight.

Second, Josh **persevered** greatly through Chicago's brutal winter and spring weather. They say that if you don't like the weather in Chicago, wait 15 minutes and it will change. Unfortunately, 15 minutes later, it was still raining. On most days that spring, Noah's Ark had a better chance of getting airborne.

The Sportstar isn't the type of aircraft that can be flown in all types of weather. It takes fairly calm conditions. As Josh's June birthday neared and he needed more flight hours, he was continually rebuffed by high winds and inclement weather. Josh never wavered. If one lesson was cancelled, instead of throwing a hissy fit, he immediately scheduled the next one. Yes, 15-year-olds still throw hissy fits. If you have one, then you know what I mean.

Josh, though, was undeterred, as he knew the end game was soloing on June 2. That's where he focused all his attention.

What about your people? How do they handle the adversity that comes along with their position? Do they persevere like Josh did, or do they throw in the towel? How do they handle a bad day? A couple of bad days? How do they handle rejection when the customer says no? When things don't go as planned? How do they handle that which they have no control over?

Third, Josh **prepared** in a way I'm unaccustomed to seeing in someone so young. You may know that all pilots prepare for their flights by reviewing (and reviewing and reviewing) a pre-flight checklist. That's the reason you see your pilot on the tarmac observing the aircraft from many different angles. Getting dirty, so to speak. Pilots of triple 7s and small aircraft alike prepare immensely for each flight, going over and over each detail that will help them land their aircraft safely.

How would you rate your team's preparation skills? Do your people prepare for each sales call? Each difficult conversation? Do they review current trends? Do they review the notes from the last meeting? Do they know the objective? Do they know what they want to accomplish on each call? Do they try to leave their people and their accounts better than before? That is, do they prepare in a way that will leave people better off as a result of time spent with them? Do they plan their days out ahead of time? A pilot files a flight plan before his flight, so he knows where he's going. Do your people choreograph their days similarly? They should!

Fourth, Josh understood his **priorities**, and we certainly helped him with that! His priority was to fly, but our priority was to make sure his grades didn't falter. Strangely, our priority became his priority. Explained another way, Josh completed his schoolwork so he could fly. The ultimate priority was maintaining a high GPA, and that's what he's done. So he was able to fly.

How do your people maintain their priorities? Do they get the essentials done so they can spend time engaging in value-added activities? Often, the obvious priorities aren't front and center. Your associates have to accomplish something else to make way for what really matters.

Finally, Josh has the most important trait of all. He has tremendous **passion** to fly. Look around his bedroom. There are flying charts all over the walls. Would you like to be more versed on restricted air space? Josh can help you. Want to learn a bit more about his airport's landing pattern? Consult the chart above his desk.

Josh doesn't have a poster of the late *Farrah Fawcett* on his wall. Wait, wrong generation. Nor does he have a poster of the cast of *Glee* or *Beyonce* or even Jill's hero *Bon Jovi*. (Ah, Jon Bon Jovi – woman want him…and men want to be like him!)

Back to Josh's bedroom walls. He does have a chart that shows where O'hare's airspace starts and ends. Is it a bit bizarre? Perhaps, but that's how he rolls.

He simply lives and breathes flying, often watching YouTube videos of hard landings at remote airports and studying aeronautical books into the wee hours (when he's not on Facebook!).

He is crazy passionate about flying.

And here's the hard question for your people: Are they passionate? Do they love what they do?

Let's examine this a bit further.

Do your people have to love the products they sell? No! Do they have to like the products they sell? Well, not really, but they do need to be passionate about their job as it relates to placing profitable products in their customers' accounts. They do have to be passionate about their customers' success, their teammates' success, and their own success. Passionate to see people soar. To see themselves soar. (I know. Corny. But it fits the theme here!)

There is simply no doubt. The **p**ractice, **p**erseverance, **p**reparation, adherence to **p**riorities, and **p**assion that Josh showed leading up to his big day made his big day possible, and it will do the same for you and your team.

That's just the way it works!

MISTAKE 28

PASSING THE TRASH

Do you *pass the trash*?

Perhaps I should explain!

I've seen many talented professionals in my travels. But I also see my fair share of unmotivated, underperforming people. I call them "space holders".

They're just taking up space.

I find that sales organizations are notorious for "*passing the trash*". Not actual garbage, mind you, but professionals who are acting (and performing), well, like garbage. Be it behavior or performance or a combination of the two, the tendency is to move these individuals around instead of moving them elsewhere (read: another place of employment).

Are you catching my drift here? Do you pass the trash? Do you think that Charlie will perform better under Paul's tutelage, when Frank's coaching and leadership couldn't do the trick? Do you get lulled into thinking that the East Side route will be better for Charlie than the West Side route?

Yes, I realize that there are personality clashes, and not all individuals (managers and employees) are destined to work together. However, moving Charlie from team leader to team leader (where he invariably creates the same disturbances) doesn't solve any problems. Rather, it only serves to exasperate the problems, both for Charlie and the organization.

So how do you handle the Charlies of the world?

Before doing anything, Charlie's manager should look in the mirror to determine if he's helping to cause the problem in any way. The truth is that managers usually have something to do with the drama they find themselves in. As a manager in a situation like this, the first move is to look in the mirror and ask yourself the following questions: (1) What can I do differently? and (2) What part of this situation has my fingerprints on it?

We certainly can't expect Charlie to change if his manager won't.

Sometimes, though, despite the best manager's best efforts, the problem turns out to be Charlie.

Then what?

I suggest you have a timely chat before the situation deteriorates to a point where communication isn't possible anymore. Do these problems typically go away? NO, and by keeping silent, you are choosing the certainty of the current situation over the uncertainty (and uncomfortable nature) of a difficult conversation.

Another litmus test: Is it ticking you off?

If yes, then, as my father-in-law says, "It's time to talk Marine to Marine!" Oddly, he has been saying this to me for twenty-five years, even though neither of us were Marines.

Say: "Could we talk about something that, if we were able to speak openly and honestly, would help you a great deal?"

Charlie will say "Yes." He may not want to, but he will.

State up front your aligned purpose. That you are both in this together. Let him know that you want to see him succeed. Highlight what you like about Charlie and his work. (Note: You should be able to find something redeeming about all your people, and if you can't, then you shouldn't have hired Charlie in the first place! Even the worst associates have some redeeming features.)

State in as positive a way as possible what you see and what you want to see. If you have to highlight past (negative) occurrences, do so and move on. Use future-based language ("in the future," "next time," "moving forward," etc.).

Offer your support to help Charlie succeed. Check for understanding. Say, "Are we on the same page?" Don't say, "Are we clear?" That's condescending. Always assume any miscommunication is due to your lack of clarity, not his lack of understanding. If Charlie needs additional training and development, see that he gets it.

Now, here's the kicker.

I learned some time ago from Jack Welch's fabulous book Winning how important being candid is to success with employees. In his book, Jack writes, "As you walk down the hallway to fire someone, if they don't know it's coming, then you haven't been candid with that person." Nobody should be shocked to be let go for performance. The handwriting should already be on the wall, in a place where they can see it.

Be candid and straightforward. Let Charlie know that you will reconvene in 60 days to reassess the situation, whereby you will make a decision on whether he has a place at the company. Be positive and show confidence, but be clear and candid. Make sure to clearly articulate goals and objectives and, most importantly, the criteria by which he will be evaluated.

Don't leave this last part out. Don't be vague by saying, "We need to see a complete turnaround." Nobody, including Charlie, will understand just how that's measured. Charlie can't work towards something that doesn't clearly exist in his mind.

Remember, you want to be fair. Others will be watching, and your treatment of Charlie will serve as an example as to how the company treats employees who need improvement.

One of three things will happen:

1) His performance will improve, leading to better times ahead.
2) His performance will not improve, meaning you will have to follow-through on your decision to help him seek employment elsewhere.
3) He will decide to seek greener pastures somewhere else. Often, this is the best outcome!

I've seen all three occurrences with my clients.

Don't waffle on having the difficult conversation. Remember, if you have a substandard person on the team, and your competitor has someone even marginally better doing the same task, they are winning in accounts, and you are losing.

And that's something that can't be tolerated in this era and this economy.

That's just the way it works.

MISTAKE 29

PRESUMING YOU CAN CHANGE
YOUR CUSTOMER'S MIND

How imaginative are your sales professionals when it comes to re-presenting a product for which their customers have already said no? Do they change things up a bit? Bring something new to the table?

As a manager, when you coach your professionals, do you stress the importance of varying their selling approach?

You should!

Recently, I sat with a young sales professional charged with selling a new tequila brand. The tequila, made from 100% blue agave, was just one dollar higher in price than its competitor, a major national brand. Suffice to say it was a good product with an attractive price.

The sales professional came up a bit short in his first try (his customer said no), and we were strategizing about how to succeed with the placement the second time around.

Before we go further, let me pose a question for you. Which of the following statements is **more accurate**?

1. You — with your infinite objection-handling skills — can easily change your customer's mind and break his or her will like a pretzel.
2. You will be more successful (the second time around) if you present new information (additional benefits, new selling approaches, and/or other interesting tidbits, etc.), and the new information will help your customer change his or her mind.

Did you choose one or two?

This is an easy one. The answer is number two!

Attention sales professionals and managers: You don't change your customers' minds. Your customers can (and may) change their minds when given more information that helps them make a confident, sensible decision.

That's why if you consistently go back to accounts saying, "Did you try the samples yet?" or "Have you reviewed my proposal?" nothing really happens.

Nothing good, anyway!

You have to come to the table with something different.

If and when you find yourself in a situation like this, I recommend the following strategy.

Say to your customer:

"Thanks for allowing me to share XYZ tequila with you again. I have to admit, I could have done a far better job presenting this to you last week, and I've done some research to create a more compelling case for you to buy."

Then share a few tangible selling benefits. Don't simply sell on price alone because (1) anybody can do it and (2) it's a terrible (overused) crutch in selling that doesn't help differentiate you from the competition. Instead, share what is different about tequilas made with 100% blue agave. Yes, they're smoother, and they taste better, but what else?

And while you're at it, consider bringing more compelling merchandising to the table. According to many experts, with busy consumers, you literally have only two seconds or so to capture their attention with your signage before they're on to the next product.

Try the following ideas for signage:

"Make one hell of a margarita, at one hell of a price!"
or
"Double the taste, without doubling the price!"

Are these sign suggestions a bit lame? Perhaps, but they're a heck of a lot better (and more informative and engaging) than a sign that says, *"100% Blue Agave Tequila"*.

So, if your people have to present a second time, make sure they vary the strategy. They're not going to *change* their customer's minds without *changing* their approach.

That's just the way it works!

MISTAKE 30

RESISTING THE NEED FOR COACHING FEEDBACK

Do you ever notice how golf shots give you instant feedback?

After your elaborate pre-swing routine, complete with much waggling of the golf club, unfortunately, you're ready to hit the ball. Almost instantly, you have some sense of what kind of shot you've hit. My buddy Rubes (who needs stronger contact lenses) automatically pipes, "That will play!" before the ball comes to a rest. The ball could be hurtling to the center of a 10,000-foot crevice, right at the base of a glacier (like in the legendary 80s movie Caddyshack), and Rubes will prematurely laud the next shot's possibilities.

For me, my next move is usually reaching into my bag for another ball (or two) before determining the best way to get past the ladies tee.

But that's golf, a sport where the ball striker gets immediate feedback, whether he wants it or not!

Not so with performance coaching.

I firmly believe in the importance of the weekly one-to-one coaching conversation. In short, I think that team leaders and managers should meet with their people at least once a week for a period of no less than 30 minutes.

This practice yields numerous benefits for both managers and the people they coach. By meeting regularly, managers will create problem-solvers. They will open the lines of communication and create more opportunities to give praise and listen attentively, leading to more discretionary effort. Additionally, managers will build more credibility with their team, as they'll be more in tune with their accounts and daily activities.

For associates, the advantages are plentiful as well. Many managers report that weekly conversations help their people become problem-solvers, which is a big part of development. I love the comments from Jack, who shared that he used to think his sales professionals saw him as the local post office. They'd stop by, drop off their problems, and assume that they'd be solved, much like how the mail seems to arrive at the logical destination. Usually!

Other managers tell me that, since they've started having weekly strategic meetings, they've developed stronger bonds, leading to better relationships and a more proactive approach to business.

So, yes, there are numerous reasons for the weekly coaching conversation, but for the purpose of this chapter, let's concentrate on the feedback process. How effective are you with your time spent coaching?

I find it helpful to ask 2 questions:

(1) How does a coach get feedback? and (2) Who measures the success of a coaching session?

The quick and uncomplicated answer is that the person being coached measures the effectiveness of the coaching. But it's more complicated than that. Many managers press me on this point. They say, "Doesn't my opinion count when determining the success of a coaching session? Don't I have a say?"

Of course, you have to be happy with the coaching process; however, I invite you to consider the following. If you (the manager) think you got your point across successfully, but your associate resembles a deer in headlights, then the session hasn't truly been a success. The person being coached determines the level of effectiveness. Does he or she feel the value of the coaching is worth more than the opportunity (or cost) of doing something else?

On the other hand, if you (the manager) feel you were off your game that day, but your associate feels *better than before*, then the session was a big success. If he or she learns some strategies with which to handle tasks, it's better for everyone. If the associate feels more able and willing to tackle responsibilities after the session than before, then the time spent was worth it, even if you (the manager) didn't accomplish all your coaching goals.

Yes, the manager's opinion counts, just not as much as the opinion of the person being coached.

Nevertheless, just asking is a great step.

Being open to feedback from your "coachee" suggests the following about your relationship:

- That you are equals
- That you can learn from one another
- That you value and respect your associate's opinion
- That you're willing to work together to improve the team's chances for success

The next important question: How does a team leader or sales manager get feedback? By asking questions, that's how, and waiting patiently for the answers.

Try asking the following:

- Do you have any feedback for me, either on today's conversation or any other conversation?
- Was this a good use of our time? What would have made it better?
- What are you taking out of this discussion?
- Was there anything you hoped we'd cover but didn't?
- On a 1-10 scale, how helpful was this to you?
- How can I improve my coaching?
- What would make these sessions more useful?
- When you saw this appointment on your calendar, how did you feel?

With the last question, we're obviously looking for a positive feeling concerning the process. If your associate gets an upset stomach from the thought of spending time with you, then, "Houston, we have a problem!"

The overall point is that successful coaching is a two-way conversation, and a great sign of respect comes from the coach soliciting and accepting feedback.

More respect equals greater acceptance of your coaching!

That's just the way it works.

MISTAKE 31

SAYING, "JUST GO GET IT DONE!"

Do you ever say, *"Just go get it done"*?

Recently, I was at a client, and I overheard a manager say the following to a sales professional.

"Just go get it done!"

He sort of barked it, and to say the young person left with a puzzled look on his face would be an understatement. Maybe the manager was thinking of the legendary Nike phrase, *Just do it,* where athletes of all abilities can suddenly scale great heights just by uttering those words...

I don't think the young man saw it that way. He saw it more as *Just do what???*

The whole scene got me thinking about the act of setting and achieving expectations.

Do you ever use that phrase? *"Just go get it done!"*

You know, when you're mired in the middle of a hundred different tasks, each seemingly more important than the last, so you tell your minions, *"Just go get it done!"*

I used to say it all the time. I'm guilty. These situations usually ended in disappointment.

I guess my question is: *Does that statement really work anymore?* I imagine that despite the fact that managers want delegating tasks to be that easy, most would agree that much more clarity is needed.

So, what's inherently wrong with the phrase?

For starters, the very statement suggests that the manager is making a ton of assumptions.

- He is assuming that the listener understands what "it" is.
- He is assuming that the listener understands the importance of "it".
- He is assuming that the listener understands how to go about getting "it" done.
- He is assuming that the listener understands why it's important to do "it".

101

- He is assuming that the listener understands when "it" should be done.
- He is assuming that the listener understands the first step towards getting "it" done.

Yes, loads and loads of assumptions and you know what they say about assumptions!

It begs the question, why do people need so much information to get "it" done?

Here's my theory. In the Internet age, we have access to so much more information than even just a few years ago. As a result, we've come to expect more information, and when we don't get answers, we're left to fill in the voids. It's an uncomfortable feeling for most. Further, we're less likely to ask questions because we're supposed to have all the answers.

We make assumptions, and our assumptions aren't always correct.

So what's the best way to handle this? I've heard it said that if you remove all the reasons why people don't do what you want, there's a much better chance that they will do what you want.

To that end, if you want tasks to get done in the manner you see fit, do the following:

1) State your expectations clearly and succinctly. Fill in the details.
2) Offer your support by providing direction, guidance, and the necessary resources.
3) Check for understanding by asking questions.

Seek to determine that your people understand your wishes and that their interpretation of your instructions is correct. Ask if there is *"anything that could get in the way of getting the task done when it's supposed to be done?"* While you're at it, make sure to specify the date you want "it" done. Yes, you're going to get some excuses, so you might as well handle them now, rather than later.

Most of all, don't assume that just because someone has been doing "it" for 20 years, that they automatically know how to do "it" correctly. If you're more thorough with your explanations, then there will be a much greater chance that they will get "it" done — correctly.

That's just the way it works.

MISTAKE 32

SCOWLING AND GROWLING

Last year, I gave a presentation, and there was a guy sitting in the second row with an intense scowl on his face the entire time. As I moved around the room, trying to establish eye contact with others in the audience, my gaze kept returning to this individual, as if drawn by a magnet.

Why was he scowling? Or growling? Was he doing both? Can you scowl and growl at the same time? I just couldn't tell.

Was it something I said? Was he trapped in an activity (my presentation) for which he had absolutely no use? Was his breakfast not agreeing with him?

Did I have what he had?

I was still searching for answers as the session ended.

Then something odd occurred.

He came right up and told me how much he enjoyed the presentation. (The fact that someone shared those sentiments is not the odd part!) The odd part is that he had seemed so unhappy the whole time.

Then I started thinking about it. Was he a "habitual scowler"? Was he like that with everybody? Could his team tell the difference between the *happy scowl* and the *unhappy scowl*?

A big mistake smart managers <u>don't</u> make is underestimating the effect of their facial expressions.

I believe that your expression says it all. That is, if you have a perpetually negative expression on your face, it can't be good for your management skills or your team's morale, for that matter.

Which brings me to the Chicago Bears' Jay Cutler. No, Jay doesn't hold a management position in a sales company, as far as I know, but his signature facial expression does carry some weight in certain circles. In the Bears' season-ending loss to the Packers in early 2011, Jay (especially after he left the game with a knee injury) wore that same indifferent look (scowl) on his face, the same face he's worn throughout the season and his career.

He just looks like he doesn't care.

Does it really matter what the public thinks about him? Not really. He's already had a successful financial career, and he's reached the pinnacle of his sport. I don't think he cares what the public thinks. His teammates? He may care what they think, but the public? Not a chance.

He doesn't have to care what other people think. But you do.

Do you wear the expression you want other people to see? You know the stats. Much more of your communication comes from what you don't say than what you do say. Things like eye contact, posture, and facial expressions say a lot about you. They're a big deal.

And the sad fact is that your people spend a lot of time trying to understand your expressions. Worse yet, that's what your associates remember — not when you greet them warmly, but when you look the other way as they approach.

They fixate on that, much like I did that day with the scowler. I focused on him. In retrospect, his behavior reminded me of the lame joke we used to tell as children: *That's so funny I forgot to laugh.*

He liked my work so much he forgot to smile.

Me? Next time I go back to "scowling man's company," I'm going to sit him in the back row.

That's just the way it works. (I get to make the seating chart!)

MISTAKE 33

SELLING WITH NO IMAGINATION

Do you look for opportunities on the edges?

Have you ever heard of a rip tide? A rip current, which many call a rip tide, occurs when strong winds and waves converge to create a dangerous undertow that pushes a swimmer away from the shore. Not that I've ever had this experience, but swimmers caught in this dangerous situation are advised by experts to swim parallel until the current weakens, which allows the swimmer to make it safely back to shore. Affected swimmers are wise to find their opportunity to return to shore by looking on the edges. That is, they must move horizontally, instead of vertically, until they find a break in the waves.

Unfortunately, as panic sets in, most try to swim directly back to shore, but that's like being on a treadmill. The swimmer doesn't go anywhere. The tragedy doesn't occur because the swimmer is sucked under; it occurs due to exhaustion from fighting a losing battle. The swimmer ultimately tires and drowns.

Recently, I was talking to a company owner who compared the sensation of a rip tide to what was going on in his business. I thought his take was ingenious. He shared that his managers, instead of using the same old strategies over and over, were trying to look at situations a little differently. The results were excellent, despite a very tough selling environment.

We all know that it's tough to grow large, mature brands. Despite their importance, I see far too many sales professionals selling these items with the same tired playbook. I liken this to being caught in a rip tide and fighting tirelessly to get back to shore. The company owner convened his team together to brainstorm new and different ideas to grow the business, instead of using, once again, the same methods to sell the same brands.

The result was incremental improvement with big brands but tremendous success with other brands and customers. By looking on the edges, they found other openings and other opportunities.

Whether it's the beginning of the year or the end, consider doing the following exercise with your team. Convene the entire team in a room with a flip chart. Yes, include everyone. In this day and age, you can't go it alone. You need contributions from everyone. Have plenty of paper. (As a side note, I think that the flip chart is one of the most underused tools for encouraging engagement and participation. Truth be told, I'm always disheartened when I return to one of my clients and see that the flip chart hasn't been used since my last visit. Is that sharing too much information?)

On the flip chart, draw a vertical line down the middle. First, ask the team to mention strategies they've used in the last year to move the needle forward (even just a little) every day. Try for as many suggestions as possible, and write every comment on the left side of your line. Make sure to include strategies that involve your selling processes, systems, customers, brands, and anything else that covers the sales and service spectrum.

This list will resemble the sensation of trying to swim back to shore in the midst of a rip tide. The harder you try to reach your goals, the farther away you get. That's what happens when you keep repeating what has worked in the past but may not be working anymore. Instead, look for little openings with your customers and with different items.

On the right side of your flip chart, list other creative ways to engage your customers and get people interested in your products. What are some strategies that haven't been tried before? What are some strategies that other companies have used with success? What are your competitors doing, within reason (and the law) that you aren't doing? Brainstorm. Come up with different ways to do what you normally do. Make sure to foster an atmosphere of acceptance, and consider the spirit with which even the silly suggestions are given. Figure it this way. A member of your team wouldn't suggest an idea if he or she didn't believe in it. Do whatever you can to discourage sarcasm and ridicule.

Write everything down, and resolve to shake it up a bit. Last but not least, make sure that managers give their opinions last, so as not to contaminate the process. You know that once a manager has spoken, everyone is just going to follow his or her lead. Ingenuity will grind to a halt in short order.

Take time to consider what you can do differently to make it back to shore, if you will. You'll be happy to be on land again.

That's just the way it works!

MISTAKE 34

SETTING A POOR EXAMPLE

From time to time, I write about my favorite *smoothie* shop. Although the smoothies are great, the service leaves a bad taste in my mouth. They constantly miss opportunities to provide great service. Accordingly, if the shop's employees are happy that I stopped by their shop, over others, it's certainly news to me.

Now I understand the problem.

The other day I ventured over as I usually do when the weather's nice.

As I entered with my son, I noticed that there were 3 people sitting in the very corner of the shop. They seemed like customers to me. I think they may have been playing cards.

There was nobody behind the counter.

Three or four minutes passed by. *"Hello?"* I offered to nobody in particular. Maybe all the employees were taking a *texting* break.

After a few more minutes a middle-aged woman got up from the corner table, went behind the counter and said in an aggravated fashion, *"Can I help you?"*

I must have interrupted her card game because she wasn't overjoyed with the prospect of helping me. Either that or maybe she had a bad hand.

Maybe she wasn't bringing down the house...

Anyway, I had never seen the woman before but I turned to my son and said, *"She's the owner. There's no doubt in my mind. She's the owner."*

My son, who, most likely couldn't have cared less, wanted to know how I knew. *"In the car!" I told him.*

I asked and sure enough she was the owner!

Now, how did I know this? How did I know she was the owner? I had never seen the woman before and I know I'm not clairvoyant.

When I tell this story, I ask the members of my group to guess how I knew. The prevailing sentiment is because she actually got up and did something. That's a good point but not the reason.

I knew because if the owner cares so little about attentive service, why should the employees. As soon as I saw the woman rise from the table (after more than 5 minutes), I knew the reason for the indifferent service.

She's setting the example, and the employees are just following her lead. They may not know any better.

She's setting an example all right. A negative example. Let's face it. If the owner of the neighborhood smoothie shop takes care of her customers in this manner, so will her employees.

You know it and I know it.

I also know the following about your role as a manager and the examples you set:

- If you blame others for everything, so will your associates.
- If you lack confidence and worry about everything, so will your associates.
- If you criticize your superiors and the company, so will your associates.
- If you run around like a chicken with your head cut off, complaining about all the things you have to do, so will your associates.
- If you do 10 things at once in a mediocre fashion, so will your associates.
- If your have fly-by-the-seat-of-the-pants organization methods, so will your associates.
- If you fail to see potential, so will your associates.

Setting a good example. Yes, it's advice all managers hear, and will never question, for it sounds so sensible, so right.

Good leaders don't file that advice away without consideration. Instead, they remember and when it's time to make a decision or act in a certain way, they make sure to set a good precedent for their people to follow.

And their people notice – and give good service. Actually, they deliver a great experience. They make the experience of buying a smoothie as wonderful as drinking it. And their customers come back again and again.

That's just the way it works.

MISTAKE 35

SIGNALING THAT YOUR PRICES ARE TOO HIGH

Deep in the recesses of terminal 3 at O'Hare International Airport, there's a little newsstand where I occasionally pick up an energy bar or newspaper before my flight. One day, I stopped by to make a purchase before leaving for Seattle. I put two energy bars on the counter, and the cashier held one up and said, "This is *$3.50...*"

Since this isn't my first rodeo, I've become accustomed to being gouged at the O'Hare for items that cost much less just a few feet away from the airport. But I have to tell you, his actions struck me – in part because the same scenario has happened to me before with the same gentleman.

That's when you know when you're traveling a lot!

Anyway, he seemed to be telling (or in this case, reminding) me that the energy bar was quite expensive. His actions were almost an apology of sorts. Perhaps he was trying to dissuade me from making the purchase.

His body language suggested that he was embarrassed. It was almost like he was hanging his head in shame. I took this as a clear signal exactly how he felt about his store's prices.

I don't know this for certain, so please grant me the privilege of a making a few assumptions based upon my retail experience. I'll bet you that this gentleman is a price shopper. My guess is that he'd never, *ever* pay $3.50 for an energy bar.

Please don't misunderstand – there's nothing wrong with any of that in one's personal life. But when it bleeds into the retail setting is when it becomes detrimental. I used to have people like this working in my business. They inadvertently sent counterproductive messages to our customers. They allowed their demeanor to signal their personal thoughts on our pricing structure.

They'd send hidden messages like, "Don't buy this," or "The price is too high," or "You can get it cheaper elsewhere."

Back at O'Hare, perhaps the clerk was saying through his subtext, "I would never buy something this expensive!"

The odd part was that the sale was already made *and* I never asked for the price.

I find two redeeming lessons from this experience. Simply put, it's a mistake to allow your people to signal that your prices are too high. The reality is that there is always going to be a cheaper price, somewhere, and it's not an associate's role (or responsibility) to signal that fact to your customers.

Consider the following two points:

First, be careful about hiring price-conscious people to interact with customers. Hire people who genuinely want to serve other people. Hire good communicators. Hire good, hardworking people. And hire people that use your product. In other words, if you're hiring at The North Face retail stores, don't bring a couch potato into the company. Hire associates who like to be outdoors and might actually wear the clothing. If you hire associates for a beverage business, look for wine, spirit and craft beer aficionados, not someone who doesn't like alcoholic beverages.

Second, since the above suggestion is extraordinarily difficult to accomplish, help your people understand that it's best to keep their opinions about price to themselves. In other words, make sure your people don't send signals, both verbal and non-verbal, to customers about the price of your products. Especially if your prices are higher than they should be!

Signals might include...

- Using language that suggests bad news is coming by saying, "you're not going to like this," "You may want to sit down for this," or similar sentiments. Or telling me the price when I didn't ask the price
- Looking down when saying the price – not establishing eye contact.
- Not saying the price clearly – maybe hoping that they won't hear you.
- Judging what might or might not make sense for the customer.

Instead, let the customer raise the objection – if there's one to be raised. State the price as you would the time.

The time is 8:30am and the price is $3.50.

So, to the manager of the newsstand at O'Hare, train your sales associates to understand that the whole point of a place to buy energy bars between gates H11 and H12 is convenience. Customers may not like it, but they understand that prices will be higher.

At the end of the day, if your associates (hold their heads up high) and show confidence in your prices no matter what they are, they won't talk customers out of making purchases.

With the proper instruction, your sales associates will help increase, not decrease, sales volumes.

That's just the way it works.

MISTAKE 36

SLIGHTING YOUR CUSTOMERS

Earlier this year, I had a meeting with a couple of young sales professionals. Usually, I'm doing the selling, but in this case, I had my checkbook out. The gentleman directly across the table from me had a brand spankin' new iPad, fresh from the Christmas holiday. As the new toy booted up, he took advantage of Starbucks' free Wifi service and accessed the Internet. I figure a five-dollar cup of coffee should come with something free, but I digress!

I assumed he needed Internet access for his presentation but I was wrong.

He needed the Web so he could check (and respond) to his email all meeting long.

Now, keep in mind that working on an iPad is a different experience from working on a laptop computer. With a laptop, a user can check his or her email, and nobody can really tell what's happening. He or she could be "un-friending" me on Facebook for all I know. The screen is hidden.

Not so with an iPad.

With an iPad, everyone at the table can see what's going on. Me? I have a raging case of ADD. I lose my train of thought like my children lose their hats and gloves. That's quickly, by the way. The other day I opened Danny's locker (at parent-teacher conferences) and a clothing store fell out.

Wait, where was I?

Oh yeah! Unavoidably, as if attracted by a magnet, I was transfixed by the guy reading his email while speaking to me about my important project. Talk about a mixed message.

And I felt slighted. And unimportant, although he was telling me how much he wanted my business. His relative indifference was sending a completely different message.

He was making a mistake that smart managers don't make. He wasn't paying attention to the person in front of him.

I wanted to say something, but we had just met. Maybe he's reading this chapter right now...on his iPad... during an important meeting.

So, the next time New Year's Day comes around, in addition to giving up dessert and other delicacies, resolve to do the following:

Pay attention!

Pay attention to the person you're meeting with and not to anyone or anything else.

Whether it's a customer, a part-time cashier or a group of sales professionals, put down your plethora of mobile devices, and share your undivided attention. It's bad out there. Really bad. Just check out most conference rooms. Everybody sets their mobiles on the table like weapons. There's lots of activity under the table, if you know what I mean. (TYPING!)

I have a buddy who, at dinner, sets his Blackberry on the table like it's part of the table setting. I think the real question is - does the Blackberry go to the right or the left of the salad fork?

Where is Miss Manners when we need her?

You know you want to. You know it's important. Could this be the year? Yes! Resolve to make it your priority.

Anyway, it sure beats hitting the health club every morning!

That's just the way it works.

MISTAKE 37

SPEEDING THROUGH RED LIGHTS

My wife and I never seem to agree on a movie we both enjoy.

She likes anything good (and serious), and me, well, the dumber the movie, the more likely I want to see it.

One of my favorites is Steve Martin's ageless classic *The Man with Two Brains*. There's a scene where the main character, Dr. Michael Hfuhruhurr (how else would you spell it?) falls in love with a beautiful woman and stands in front of a large wall portrait of his late wife to seek her approval.

He wants her to show him a "sign" if it's not ok to see the new woman.

The portrait (and everything in the house) starts shaking, spinning around and around and around, and a woman's voice cries out, "No, no, no, no, no, no!"

She sends quite a sign.

When the shaking stops and the dead woman's cries cease, Dr. Hfuhruhurr asks again, "Just give me any sign, and I won't see the new woman ever again." Too funny!

Anyway, I guess you had to be there! I find it to be a hilarious scene, and it's probably part of the reason why Jill and I can't seem to agree on which movie to see on Saturday night, or any other night for that matter.

In the scene, our oblivious hero misses an obvious sign, which begs the following questions…

Do you ever miss obvious signs? Do you ever miss an obvious sign from a customer? From an associate?

Recently, I coached a young manager who had a similar experience, although not so dramatic.

She was selling a new product from a long-standing national supplier. Her customer's reaction was quite visceral. "No, no, no. I don't want to carry any of their stuff." It wasn't the typical "I don't have space…" objection or other similar sentiment. Our heroine, like many, many before her, didn't miss a beat. She kept selling. She listened less and talked more, possibly hoping to *out benefit* the guy into submission. Perhaps she thought she could browbeat the customer into changing his mind.

Unfortunately, she missed an opportunity, a chance to step back and learn something about her customer.

One of my basic tenets is that a manager, associate and sales professional should learn something new about his or her customers on each visit. After the call, he or she should reflect on the question, Did I learn anything about my customer on this visit? If the answer is no, then he or she should prepare differently for the next visit. Sometimes, it helps to have a few good questions in your hip pocket.

The young manager should have stopped on a dime and traded the fleeting opportunity to place the product (that day) for a better outcome — learning something valuable about the customer.

If you ever find yourself in that position, do the following:

Say, "That was quite a reaction. Do you mind if I ask why you feel so strongly about these brands?"

Or try saying, "So that I may serve you better in the future, may I ask why you feel so strongly?"

Choose your own words, but ask the question.

Your customer will like the fact that you've shelved your own agenda to get inquisitive and to be a better listener. It shows you actually care, instead of just acting like you do. Armed with what you learn, you can always try again for the placement next week. Your chances for success then will be much better.

Also, just because I've used a sales example in this chapter doesn't mean that this mistake doesn't occur every day between managers and their people. My favorite was a quick note I got from a sales professional who told me that after weeks of disappointing sales, he finally told his manager, "He was sucking wind lately!"

The manager's reply, "That must be very difficult..." and then he moved on to the next item on his agenda.

Talk about blowing through a red light.

The sales professional was devastated. Talk about a cry for help! If there ever was an opportunity to learn something about your team member, that chance was hand delivered with a ribbon on it.

But the manager never even slowed. He ran the red light and never looked back. If you do the same, with customers or associates, they won't look back, either, as they take their needs elsewhere.

That's just the way it works!

MISTAKE 38

SQUANDERING VALUABLE TIME

I could have titled this chapter, "Wasting time on people who don't give a frogs fat booty about you."

Or I could have started it with a theoretical question. Is managing your time a cold-blooded activity?

Yes, managing your time successfully is a cold-blooded activity. Why "cold-blooded"? Well, as you might have heard, there are only so many hours in the day. You heard that one – right? Time is at a premium, but that doesn't stop managers from squandering time. Many managers are naturally drawn to what's easy and more comfortable, which, in turn, usually causes one to be less productive.

Yes, choosing how to allocate your time (if you take the process seriously) is simple but certainly not easy! It's simple because you know what to do. You know, intrinsically, that you should concentrate on activities that move you closer to your goals, but it's not easy because of all the distractions. For example, Reality TV has made wasting time a realistic goal for most people.

The Internet has made wasting time a realistic goal for the rest.

Since we're talking about wasting time, I remember lying in bed one Saturday morning and reading the news on my iPhone. I saw a story about the reality show Jersey Shore. Before I go any further, let me say that I'm not a big fan of reality TV, except for the Biggest Loser, which I find motivating. I watch that show religiously, usually while enjoying a bowl of ice cream...

...With whip cream.

Anyway, I saw a story about the "star" (I use the term loosely) of Jersey Shore, *Snooki*. I wouldn't know *Snooki* if she was sitting across the table from me, but I was tempted to click on the link and read the story. Why? I have no idea! Then I caught myself, got out of bed in a huff, and sat down to do some writing. Doing anything constructive would've been an improvement. Why should I waste my time reading about the trials and tribulations of *Snooki*? Would *Snooki* waste her time learning about the trials and tribulations of me?

I know my family finds me fascinating...

I mean, I think they do.

But, *Snooki*; I wouldn't think so. She's has big hair and my hair has been in *recession* for many years.

Similarly, how does watching a YouTube video of a cat doing a backwards somersault get you any closer to your goals? It doesn't, and that's why being productive is a cold-blooded activity. By the way, I was presenting to a group of sales professionals recently when I made an offhand comment to a young man in the front row: "When you watch a silly YouTube video of a cat doing a somersault, you never get the time back."

To this, he replied, "I'm not getting this time back either!"

Ouch.

I guess you have to have ice running through your veins to not give a hoot about acrobatic felines and/or "The Situation". (Is he *Snooki's* friend?)

Never mind! Does anyone really care?

Well, yes, people do care but I hope you're not one of them because they're not going to help you pay your mortgage and put food on the table.

They're certainly not going to help you develop your people.

In all seriousness, the choice is yours to make better use of your time and be better organized with your activities. The choice is yours to spend your time in high-value activities. To spend time on activities that are, both urgent, and important.

Stay away from time-wasting reality stars whose only interest in you is you spending your hard-earned cash on their overpriced clothing and fragrance lines. And don't even get me started on Ashton Kutcher and Demi Moore. As of this writing, they've tweeted devastating news. Their marriage is over. Irreconcilable differences.

Is that what the locals call adultery these days?

By the way, I think I just "teared" up a little – I really thought those kids were going to make it work.

There are 12 Million people are following these bozos on Twitter. Imagine if a few of their followers picked up a book one in a while.

Are you following Ashton and Demi? (And now is not the time to choose sides. We should support them both unconditionally.)

But, really, please don't be one of those people. Yes, it's ok to have an outlet; a guilty pleasure of sorts – like chocolate. Or lavender bath salts... Or pickles...

Never mind! Look, I know that work and life are challenging to say the least. It's when the wasted time outweighs the productive time...

...That's when you and I have irreconcilable differences.

If you're wasting your time caring about people who don't care about you, then you're wasting time, period. And you never get that time back.

Conversely, the more organized and ruthless you are, the more time you'll have to spend with your team and your customers. You'll be more available. You'll be a better listener and a better coach. You'll probably be more organized and more professional in how you go about your duties. Probably be more *well read* and more knowledgeable about your products and industry.

Best yet, you'll cross off a major mistake that smart managers don't make - *Wasting your time on people who don't care about you.* Everyone will perform better, and the time you do spend will be well worth it.

That's just the way it works. (On second thought, maybe I should care what *Snooki* is doing. She's quite good at marketing herself. If she can give a commencement speech at Rutgers University, she could probably help me sell some of these books!)

MISTAKE 39

SQUASHING DREAMS

My middle son Danny has come a long way. Recently, he had two buddies sleep over. After one of the boys left, he whispered to me – "Now I have to get the other one out of here!

I need my down time!" (It must have been hard to sleep with the Xbox on all night…)

Anyway, when he was younger, he used far less tact. He'd say to Jill, "I want *they* to leave."

His friend could've been standing right there but that didn't seem to stop him.

He's so grown up now. Not only does he use better grammar, but also with age, he's come to realize that he doesn't have to announce every thought that enters his mind. (Except when he's being punished. In that case, he usually shares everything on his mind – and then some.)

Anyway, do you always share what's on your mind?

Hmmm…

Recently, I had an interesting chat with a team leader. Before I share our discussion, I'd like to ask you a question.

Let's say you have an associate who thinks he or she is management material, but you believe the night-shift janitor (or virtually anyone else) is a better candidate. Is it your responsibility to tell the individual how you feel? Do you have to be a straight shooter? Do you have to level with him or her? Do you have to tell him that he's not going to make it to management level?

The team leader, Terry, felt he had to level with Ramon and tell him that he wasn't management material. Do you agree?

I don't.

If Ramon's goal is to be a manager and you tell him that's not a possibility, you're effectively killing his spirit. You're certainly not leaving him *better than before*. (As always, your goal is to have Ramon leave the conversation feeling better, not worse, about himself.) After hearing such negative news, Ramon may certainly keep working at his average level, but what incentive does he have to stretch himself to do better?

119

I'll handle the tough questions.

He has no incentive.

I say you turn it into a positive. Obviously, Ramon is falling short in certain areas. Say to him, "If you improve in these areas, you will move closer to the management track." Who are you to say that Ramon won't improve his game by making the necessary changes? It's not your place. You don't get to decide; he decides. You may have a hand in deciding if he gets promoted, but you don't decide whether or not he'll make the changes necessary for consideration.

Unfortunately, every day managers live in the future, instead of the present, and make decisions unilaterally to quash their people's spirits.

Is it okay to tell Ramon that he has a ton of work to do if he wants to realize his managerial dreams?

Yes.

Is it okay to tell Ramon that he has to make some changes to be a stronger candidate?

Absolutely!

Is it ok to tell Ramon that it might be a few years before he's strongly considered for a management position?

Yes, but never act like his inability to rise to the management level is a *fait accompli*.

As you form your thoughts, consider what really needs to be said and what can be left unsaid. Be very clear on what Ramon needs to do. Concentrate on specific actions that will move the ball forward. Lay out a plan for him.

If he improves, fantastic! You're helping groom a future leader. If he stays the same, that's his decision. He's made his bed and now he gets to sleep in it. Whether he has a down comforter or a Wal-Mart fleece is up to him.

That's just the way it is!

MISTAKE 40

STARTING A FITNESS ROUTINE
BY RUNNING A MARATHON

You don't start a fitness regimen by running a marathon – do you?

More on that in a bit, but first, I have a question. Do you ever wonder what other people think about you?

Is this news you can use? Absolutely! It should be of great interest to you. Some of you may be thinking, "I don't want to know!" Uh, probably not a good idea. This chapter is about taking a good, hard look at how your people see you, and I'll begin that process by suggesting a few questions you should ask or at the very least want to know the answers to. The goal will be to find ways to ask these questions on a regular basis to your associates.

Think about it this way. Have you ever started a new fitness regimen? Typically, if you are a new exerciser, over a certain age (35 or so), and have been sedentary in your lifestyle, it is recommended that you consult a doctor first, not toe the line at the nearest marathon. The goal is to start with the right plan, one that takes your health into consideration. Younger people have it a bit easier. Their major decision is what color shorts to wear and what to listen to on their iPod.

The point is that everybody has to start somewhere.

As you start the relationship-building process with your associates, it's helpful to know where you stand.

Start by asking:

- "What am I doing well?"
- "What could I do better?"

You could also ask:

- "What should I start doing?"
- "What should I stop doing?"
- "What should I continue doing?"

It's not so much which questions you ask, but that you ask how your people see you. Do so in whatever manner you find comfortable.

One quick caveat, though. Don't ask the questions if you're going to automatically dismiss the answers. In other words, the more serious you are, the more beneficial the process will be. Automatically dismissing what others say will do more harm than good. "Denial" isn't just a river in Egypt, as they say. Besides, if your associates and customers point out the same issues, take the lesson and run with it. The truth is that if it walks like a duck and talks like duck…well, you know how that one ends.

One final thought on this subject. It doesn't matter what you think. What matters is what the people you work with on a regular basis think. Be strong, ask the questions, and the answers will help you in the long run – whether it's a trip around the block or the local marathon.

That's just the way it works!

MISTAKE 41

TAKING THE EASY WAY OUT

Not too long ago, something dawned on me. I was tired of my iPhone.

I was – I admit it. The phone is cool and all, but occasionally my roving eye sees an Android or a Blackberry and I find myself lusting after a new device. Okay, perhaps "lusting" is a bit strong, but my feelings were such that I found myself at the AT&T store one day.

I explained the details of my unimaginable dilemma to the young salesperson. I'm sure he could see that I was hot for something new, since I was practically begging him to sell me something.

Ignoring the obvious and easy sale, he calmly asked me what I liked and didn't like about the iPhone. Then he asked me four or five more questions before I concluded that the cost of changing was too high – both financially and otherwise.

After my revelation, he told me, "75% of iPhone owners who trade in Apple's finest device return within a week groveling for their old phone back!"

His honesty was really mind-boggling – as was his ability to play with my emotions.

I left the store with a new case (but not a new phone) and a newfound respect for this great young salesperson. I also managed to keep a few extra bucks in my pocket – which meant I could justify a stop at Starbucks on the way home!

He helped me see something that I didn't want to see, and that ability is a skill that every manager needs for success.

In turn, he didn't commit a mistake that smart managers don't make.

He didn't take the easy way out.

Smart managers help their people recognize the reality of their situations. Through my coaching, I've come to see that many managers are good at pointing out the reality, but not as proficient at helping their associates see reality for themselves.

Quick example: if Dan is staying out late partying and thus he can't get up early enough the following morning to be productive, that's a reality he needs

123

to accept. Sure, you can tell him, but if you ask him questions and he comes to that conclusion on his own, it's a much better situation. (Note: I'd wait until Dan's hangover subsides before having that conversation…)

Really, though, why is this important?

Well, for there to be any meaningful change, it is imperative for your associates to arrive at conclusions on their own accord. You can certainly say what needs to be said, but if there is no inherent reason for them to stop a behavior or start a new one, there is little chance for lasting improvement.

One quick note: Asking questions to help your people admit their weaknesses and/or areas of improvement is hard work. It takes longer and requires a great deal more patience, which is why so many managers take the easy way out. That is, they say *what needs to be said* instead of helping their people say *what needs to be said*. The latter is much better than the former.

Here are a few questions to help you in your efforts to help your employees recognize the reality.

Are you determining future impact?

A typical coaching topic is in convincing an associate to stop a current behavior and start a new one. One key in this process is helping associates see the future implications of their own behavior. Simply ask, "If we're talking 6 months from now and nothing has changed, what might you be telling me about this situation?"

Here's my goal with this question. If one's behavior (or performance) is such that an employee might be urged to find work elsewhere, but he or she is oblivious to that possibility, then his or her reality is distorted. A manager, who doesn't help the individual recognize the reality, is taking the easy way out.

It's best to help your people see the consequences of their actions.

Are you committing to action?

What do your people do when they find themselves in onerous situations and there seems to be nowhere to turn? Do they expect sympathy?

That's usually when their inner victim comes out to play. Do you ever have the unenviable task of coaching individuals who make every excuse under the sun to justify their inability to act?

By the way, I once worked with a manager who was so sympathetic; I thought I was at a Hallmark convention…

I felt like I needed to keep a box of tissues nearby.

Anyway, if you find yourself in a situation like that, try to get your associate to do something productive. Say, "Given your situation, as difficult as it might be, what can you do to move forward?" Create a deadline for action. Ask when you can follow up. Don't give advice as that creates dependency. Don't discount their problems or get caught up in their stories. Try not to be judgmental. Help your associates understand an alternative course of action.

Other useful questions to ask them:

- How do you see this situation?
- What is happening?
- What is working well?
- What makes this challenging?
- How might you have contributed to this situation?
- How might others see this?
- If the shoe were on the other foot, how would this feel/seem?
- What impact is this having on you?
- What are the long-term implications?
- What are the consequences if the situation doesn't change?

The key with any of these questions, from a coaching and leadership perspective, is to explore your associate's point of view **before** sharing your own. The idea is to suspend a judgmental and all-knowing attitude. Instead, be patient and maintain a mindset of curiosity. Most importantly, resist giving advice, as that act alone sabotages all your efforts for developing self-reliant associates.

In my case, what the phone salesperson did so effectively was to help me understand the situation as well as the issue and costs of changing versus not changing. And he did all that by simply asking me a few questions at a time when he could have taken the easy route: selling me something else.

He helped me see my reality.

And it's a good thing he didn't because, as of this writing, the iPhone 4S is out with the new digital assistant, Siri. She and I are doing just fine and, thanks to my new iPhone, I'm quite sure that we'll be living happily ever after!

That's just the way it works.

MISTAKE 42

TALKING TOO MUCH

I haven't run a marathon since 2002, but I still follow the Bank of America Chicago Marathon on TV every year.

Yes, I'm the one. I'm trying to keep the ratings up.

Anyway, I caught the beginning of the 2011 race on the radio during my morning trip to Starbucks. Talk about riveting radio! I actually felt bad for the announcers who had the unenviable task of describing the action – or lack thereof.

But that didn't stop them from filling the airwaves with their thoughts because that's the nature of radio. The announcers speak, and the listeners listen. For a few minutes, they spoke about the previous year's winner, Kenyan runner Sammy Wanjiri, who died tragically in a fall from his apartment balcony.

The announcer, in a comment I'm sure he'd like to take back, remarked that Wanjiri wouldn't be available to run this year.

Really? Is it because he's no longer with us? I guess I should have placed my bet differently.

Now before you accuse me of splitting hairs (which I'm doing), let me say that I know he made a simple mistake. I chalk it up to the announcer having to say something to fill the void, and not knowing exactly what to say.

And I immediately thought of managers and the conversations they have on a daily basis with their professionals. I thought of how managers think they have to talk to fill the void and how that's really not the case.

Many managers have shared that they abhor silence because it's uncomfortable and doesn't feel natural. Consequently, they try to fill the void with their words.

And the words often come out wrong.

So, is there a solution?

I believe so. When I work with managers, there's a reason why I implore them to ask questions and let the silence do the heavy lifting. I want them to open their mouths less because I know that the more a manager talks, the greater likelihood there is for the foot-in-mouth scenario.

This fact was underscored by a role-playing exercise I did with a group of managers recently. The objective was to frame a potentially unpleasant conversation. The objective of framing a conversation is to introduce, specify and gain agreement on the parameters of a conversation. I suggest this so that managers may gain agreement on the purpose and process of moving forward from the person with whom they are speaking (and to gain engagement with them as well). Framing the conversation is a tremendously respectful way to broach a difficult subject, as it gives both parties a much better chance for a productive outcome.

To spice up the exercise, I had the sales professional be less than cooperative. My goal was for the manager to stay focused on gaining agreement for the conversation to proceed – and nothing else. Often, at the first sign of defensiveness from the other party, managers will rev up their engines and start in with opinions and other innuendo.

But for managers to be successful, they must stay on-message, no matter what the professional says or does.

The results of this exercise were interesting, to say the least. The more words the manager used, the worse it got. The manager almost always veered off-message. The urge was to start asking questions and to share advice and opinion. On the other hand, the managers who were more economical with their words fared much better. They didn't get tongue-tied as quickly. They didn't say stupid things. They didn't let their ego get in the way. They didn't share their opinions, which, in my estimation, is probably the number one reason why difficult conversations become even more strained.

They stayed on-message.

Talking too much is a mistake that smart managers don't make!

As you navigate tough conversations, remember that the first thirty seconds are critical. You can't measure success within that time frame, but you can count on a greater chance for failure if there are too many unnecessary comments and not enough planning.

So, if you want to avoid this pitfall, prepare to ask more questions and speak less than 25% of the time. Listen with mindfulness and sincerity. Use fewer words and there is a greater likelihood you won't *run* into trouble.

That's just the way it works.

MISTAKE 43

TELLING, NOT ASKING

Last 4th of July in Chicago, in addition to all the holiday festivities, the Cubs and White Sox faced each other to finish this year's Crosstown Classic. We were in the car listening to the White Sox flagship station when the Cubs (our team) hit a towering home run to tie the game..

As the Cubs had just *gone yard*, you could clearly hear the disappointment in the announcers' voices. Hawk Harrelson, the Sox's long time announcer, seemed on the verge of tears.

Being that we're Cubs fans, we flipped quickly to the Cubs broadcast and heard a distinctly different reaction. The announcers were happy, almost giddy.

You have to understand, nothing really good ever happens to the Cubs.

Anyway, the home run (a singular event) was greeted with two completely different reactions.

Later the White Sox homered and their announcers reacted exactly how you'd expect.

Of course, the Cubs lost the game on a wild pitch in the bottom of the 9th, but you probably saw that coming.

This situation reminded me that people often react to the same set of circumstances in completely different ways, and this dynamic affects all managers.

Consider the following:

Let's say you walk thru an account with your sales professional and, in your view, the place is a complete disaster. Your 9-year-old daughter could do a better job. And she only sees out of one eye. Now, it should be obvious, but let's imagine, for a second, that the sales professional doesn't see it that way.

Strangely, he thinks the account looks pretty darn good.

It's just like the Cubs/Sox reaction from above. The same set of circumstances, but a completely different reaction.

So what do you do? Well, you might get angry and let the sales professional have it, a strategy that usually ends up being counter-productive.

Instead, ask "How would you rate our execution in this account on a scale of 1 to 10?"

Asking this question serves two purposes?

First, the answer will give you an idea of how your sales professional views what you both just saw. It answers the question – do you see what I see? Just this realization alone may stop you from jumping to conclusions, which doesn't serve anyone's purpose.

Second, understanding your sales professional's insight will give you a great starting point towards skill development. After the sales professional gives his performance, or lack thereof, a score, your follow-up question is simply – "What do we have to do to get to a 10?"

Or "What can we do to move the needle forward?"

Or "What can we do differently to achieve better execution?"

The score is almost irrelevant. What matters is the answers to these questions. What matters is how to improve.

The reality is that many sales professionals don't see what you see; they see something completely different. That's why proceeding with inquisitiveness is the way to go. Ask questions. Work more with what you learn, rather than what you think you already know.

Any (and all) conversations will go much more smoothly.

That's just the way it works.

MISTAKE 44

THINKING ALL CUSTOMERS ARE THE SAME

Let me start this chapter with a statement. Six words that could blow the lid off everything you've ever learned about serving customers!

All customers are not created equally!

Let me explain by asking a few questions!

Do you have one customer who is more important than the others? Are a handful of customers more important than the others? Do certain customers have more strategic importance?

Of course, the official company line is no! Treat everyone the same! They're all important! That's what we tell our people. After all, that's one of the great foundations of success in sales and customer service. Right? Treating everyone with the highest level of service and respect.

Well, yes and no. Yes, the goal is to treat everyone the same, but in practice, that's quite difficult, due to the often overwhelming amount of responsibilities being placed on sales and management professionals and the increasing amount of time needed to manage accounts properly.

Unfortunately, I spend a lot of time talking to managers about execution breakdowns. These are situations in which sales professionals and other employees fail to fulfill key expectations. Situations where a major account doesn't survive inspection. Maybe it's a big-shot buyer making the rounds or a supplier coming to town. Whatever the case, the account isn't as prepared and pristine as everyone had hoped, and people aren't happy.

Strike that. People are actually very unhappy!

So I ask, "As this particular account (or location) is so important, did you communicate, confirm, check, and re-check compliance with the applicable sales professional?"

And I hear, "We sent out an email." Or "We mentioned it at a meeting."

Unfortunately, when managers rely on these methods of communication, they are putting their faith in big-time assumptions. These managers are assuming that their sales professionals are listening and that they're reading all their emails.

Not exactly an accurate depiction of reality.

Most people don't read all their emails, and they certainly aren't always listening. So if they get 50% of what you say (or write), which parts are they getting?

Are they getting the important parts?

When a manager tells me that he or she sent an email, or similar, I reply, "Yes, but did you communicate, confirm, check, and re-check this particular location because of its relative importance in the food chain?"

And they reply, "Shouldn't it be done because I emailed or mentioned it? Do I have to specifically mention certain key accounts? Shouldn't all the accounts be maintained properly? Do I have to be that specific?"

Yes!

In theory, all accounts should be treated with the same level of importance; however, the most effective managers endlessly communicate, confirm, check, and re-check the ones that matter the most. High-volume accounts or those businesses with the most visibility. Maybe even the location right on the buyer's preferred route home.

The funny part is that the misses will be invariably at big, important accounts like mass discounters or grocery stores, accounts where one would suspect that smarter heads would prevail. It's not the businesses like Pete's Roadside Grocery that get people in trouble.

It's the Walmarts of the world.

And when things fall through the cracks like this, it hurts employee engagement because it's a negative occurrence. Conversely, with fewer misses, there are more reasons to celebrate with positive activities that help strengthen relationships.

Celebrations are good for all the *parties* involved.

So, yes, the mantra to the team is that all retailers are created equal. Treat the big as you would the small. The important as you would the unimportant. After all, one day, Pete's Roadside Grocery may rise up and become an important player.

But for best success, though, remember the 4 Cs when it comes to performance and execution where it matters the most. Make sure to communicate, confirm, check, and re-check, and less will fall through the cracks.

Especially with those accounts where you can least afford breakdowns in execution.

Yes, all your customers are not the same.

That's just the way it works.

MISTAKE 45

TOLERATING COMPLACENCY

October of 2011 was a pretty exciting time to be a Cubs fan.

I know that's a strange thing for a Cubs fan to say, but I was pretty enthused by the arrival of Theo Epstein, one of the architects of the great Boston Red Sox teams of the last several years. He's the new leader of the Cubs' baseball operation. Just after he was hired, I heard him interviewed on the radio.

He was asked about the Red Sox's epic collapse at the end of the 2011 baseball season. You may remember that they blew a huge lead (in September) and failed to make the playoffs. Shortly after the season, it was revealed that some players were behaving quite poorly while in uniform. Rumor has it they were drinking beer and eating fried chicken in the clubhouse — during games!

His (Theo's) answer: They (management) had grown complacent after the team's red-hot start.

They took their eye off the ball, if you will.

They tolerated complacency, and in doing so, they missed the playoffs, a big no-no in the Red Sox nation.

As I listened, I thought about complacency and its ugly effect on business. To help you avoid tolerating complacency, I suggest that you contemplate the following 9 questions. As you review these questions, you'll notice that many cover subjects are so important that I've dedicated a whole chapter in *Table for Three?* to them,

I hope you answer honestly! Answering honestly will help you determine whether you're hitting it out of the park or striking out on 3 pitches. Yes, we're going with a baseball theme in this chapter!

1.   Are you showing enough appreciation?

Do your people feel that you're taking them for granted? Do they feel that you value their work? Not everyone likes to be appreciated in the same way. Some like verbal encouragement, while others like help with their duties every once in a while. Or they may like small gifts or tokens of appreciation. Whatever the case, you won't know the preferred method unless you ask. Don't make the mistake of assuming that everyone wants to be recognized in the same manner. The success of your appreciation efforts will clearly be in the eye of the beholder.

2.   Are you learning enough about your people?

In other words, are you still learning about the people you manage and lead? Are you still curious (and eager to learn more) about people you may already know very well? Are you curious about those individuals you know nothing about?

It's tempting to think you know it all, but do you?

3. Are you asking enough questions?

Are you actively looking for ways to keep the conversation going? I once heard the following phrase once: The question is the answer. I believe it. Asking questions is a much better way to go because you learn more by listening, than by talking. *You already know, what you know.* The key is what does the other person know. That's what you should be trying to figure out.

Keep in mind that the less you talk, the more you hear. The more you listen, the more you know.

4.   Are you sharing your undivided attention?

Are you looking people straight in the eye, or are you reading email while your associates are talking to you? Maybe it's ok to multitask while working on your computer (although few experts think it's effective), but it's not ok with your people.   You're not bringing your smart phone to lunch – are you?

4. Are you having difficult conversations when need be?

Many managers abhor broaching sensitive topics. They choose the uncertainty of an unresolved (and potentially negative) situation over the certainty that comes with approaching your associate to talk about a touchy subject. It's certain to be uncomfortable. It shouldn't be a great surprise that avoiding difficult conversations rarely leads to any improvement.

5. Are you clearly sharing your key expectations?

Does your team know a key expectation from a regular expectation? (Please don't say that they're all equal. They're not! You know it, and I know it!) Are you taking the time to determine whether your expectations are reachable? Are you taking the time to determine what's involved before asking your people to do something?

7.   Are you looking in a real mirror?

Many managers spend a lot of time looking for a mirror that tells them exactly what they want to hear while avoiding any reflection that presents an unflattering picture. Managers who fall prey to this illusion fail to recognize that they usually have some role in the dramas they find themselves in. They're usually at fault in some way. Not all the time, but enough to make a difference. Accepting a more true assessment is a good step in the right direction!

8.   Are you truly coaching your people?

Judging by the answers I get when I ask managers about their coaching efforts, you'd think that every last one of them has been trained in how to maximize their performance coaching efforts. Too often, their efforts remind me of the stereotypical football coach or Army drill sergeant — lots of telling people what to do and how to do it. No! Effective performance coaching is about helping your people solve their own problems. It's about resisting the all-too-common urge to give advice at the drop of a hat.

9.   Are you leaving your people *better than before*?

Every touch point with your team is a chance to leave them *better than before*. Better able to sell than before. Better able to share your products confidently than before. Better able to provide great service than before. A better asset to the company than before. Better in at least one distinguishable way than before.

The curse of complacency is a bad, bad omen. You could say it's a harbinger for things to come, but if you ask these 9 questions (of yourself) on a regular basis, it's unlikely that you will strike out.

That's just the way it works!

MISTAKE 46

UNDERMINING YOUR SUBORDINATES

I've been with my wife, Jill, for a long, long time. She'd say "too long," but I count it at just over 27 years. (The boys say she felt sorry for me but that's a story for another day.)

Anyway, in our illustrious time together, which began in high school, I've never seen her order something off a restaurant menu without making a whole slew of changes. She'll take a salad and make so many changes, it comes out looking like a hamburger.

Seriously, though, sometimes I nod off when she's ordering! Thank goodness for smart phones.

(Yes, I know one of the main premises of this book is not using your smart phone during meals with significant others (including your employees, sales professionals and associates)... However, it takes her a really, really long time to order!)

Anyway, one night, we had dinner with another family, and our friend Susan ordered a salad and made just a few changes. After what seemed like an eternity, the salad was delivered to our table with the wrong ingredients, and despite the valiant efforts of our delightful server, the chef's second effort at getting it right wasn't much better.

When the manager stopped by, we expressed some dissatisfaction, and he promptly offered to remove it from our bill.

He did the right thing, but apparently, the master chef didn't agree. When the bill came, we noticed that we were charged for the salad.

So we asked our server. She told us that the manager had been overruled.

Ouch!

The chef had decided on a completely different resolution — no resolution!

Huh? Did it play out like a courtroom drama? "Objection! I find for the customer! Overruled!"

And the reason for the judge's decision? I guess we made too many changes.

Well, the chef came out with his silly, poufy hat, and we protested. It was almost like we were told to "talk to the hand". Our comments fell upon deaf ears. (Maybe the poufy hat was covering his ears.) If we didn't like it, we were dismissively invited to call the owner the following day.

"Have it out with her," he told us.

The chef actually made many mistakes that evening and, based upon this escapade, I'd like to share two suggestions with you.

1)   Don't discard customers!

I don't care how busy you are. You simply don't throw customers out like brown lettuce. As fickle as the restaurant business is, when a customer has chosen to spend money with you, treat it as a big deal – even if you've successfully occupied the same corner for 30 years.

You simply respect that customers have choices, and they've chosen you. Especially when money is harder to come by. Further, as a restaurateur, if you don't like patrons making changes, as stupid as that approach would be, don't allow them. So much for making guests feel welcome!

Good luck with that strategy! Next...

2)   Don't undermine a subordinate's authority!

Afterwards, the manager was nowhere to be found. Perhaps he was sent home, or he slinked away in embarrassment. We'll never know what transpired. Looking back, I can't overemphasize the damage that was done. He (the manager) had come over to the table to placate our party. He did the right thing. To have the chef go back on the restaurant's word was rude, inconsistent, and very poor customer service. And bad management

The chef was a real *weenie*. I could have profiled him in chapter 1!

So as we make our way to the end of this chapter, let me ask you...

Do you ever undermine your subordinates' authority?

As a retailer, I saw this happen all the time. A sales professional would promise one thing, and a manager would deliver quite another thing. Often, this was caused by a lack of communication. Other times, it seemed contrived and intentional. In other words, the manager would bring "a better deal," thus rendering the sales professional almost useless. You could see the life drain out of the sales professional's face. Totally deflated is how I'd describe his or her demeanor. It was like he or she wanted to disappear.

And it was embarrassing and uncomfortable for all the parties involved.

It was a condescending way to do business, as if we didn't know what was going on.

And speaking of condescending, I hope our chef the other night enjoys whipping up his special "inflexible salad" for lots of other customers.

He won't be making it ever again for our family.

That's just the way it works.

MISTAKE 47

WAITING FOR SOMEONE ELSE TO TAKE INTIATIVE

Do you ever read the advice columns in your local newspaper?

I do from time to time, and in the Chicago Tribune recently, I read an interesting post in the "Ask Amy" column. An advice-seeker wrote something to this effect:

"Why can't air travelers distinguish their black luggage, in some noticeable way, so they pull the correct bag off the carousel? I'm tired of other people grabbing my bag!"

The answer was swift and rather obvious: "Why don't you decorate your bag in some noticeable way, so that no one else would dare do the unthinkable and grab your bag?"

Amy then went into a rant about how (in today's society) it's always up to someone else and that most people don't want to take accountability for their own actions. They'd rather wait for someone else to do it. She concluded her comments by saying that shifting blame and shielding oneself from accountability seems to be the "New American way"!

I couldn't agree more and managers are not exempt. Waiting for someone else to take the initiative is a mistake that smart managers <u>don't</u> make.

Do you ever see (or feel) the following?

- Your people don't seem to get it.
- Your people can't specify their next logical action after you ask them to do something.
- You're consistently disappointed by the results people deliver.
- You often seem to get a bunch of excuses.
- After the fact (and after expectations have gone unmet), you often have to re-explain and re-clarify what you really want.

Or worse, do your people look like they're walking through fog?

Perhaps you should look in the mirror and include yourself in the accountability equation. That is, instead of blasting your people for their failure to execute, ask yourself some hard questions.

139

Look in the mirror, if you will.

Take the initiative.

The following questions will get you started, and there are plenty more where these came from: (Note: I've covered this in other parts of this book. It's important. That's why I'm repeating myself.)

- Am I being clear enough about what I expect?
- Am I being definite enough on exactly **when** I expect what I expect?
- Am I looking below the surface for the hidden thoughts and feelings that my people may not want to tell me?
- Am I offering enough support?
- Am I sharing **why** I'm asking someone to do something?
- Am I checking for understanding and next steps before sending my people on their way?
- Am I ferreting out the excuses early on in the process so I don't have to do so after the deadline has passed?

If you do include yourself in the accountability process, you (as the manager) will also see many benefits.

- You will have more positive relationships.
- Your people will listen to you more.
- You will learn from what went wrong, because you're not automatically blaming someone else.
- You will help your people get the process back on track, sooner rather than later.
- You will help create a better culture at your company.
- You will create a more positive work environment (and encourage others to do their best), because you see yourself as part of the process.
- Your people will come to you with issues, opportunities, and concerns, instead of automatically going to their friends, colleagues, family members, or worse yet, the local barista!

And as a result of all of these positive actions...

...Execution, results, and the atmosphere at your company will improve because...

That's just the way it works!

MISTAKE 48

WASTING OPPORTUNITIES
TO INFLUENCE YOUNG PEOPLE

What's the famous line? These boots were made for walking? Thanks to the Internet, I now know that Nancy Sinatra coined these semi-famous words that unexpectedly applied to me last June. My wife and I were spending a weekend in Nashville, Tennessee. On Saturday, I spent the day with a group of managers and Jill walked around town. I wonder who had more fun that day?

Anyway, while I was presenting, she happened upon a boot store with a buy one, get two free offer.

For some reason, she thought I'd be interested in a pair of my very own cowboy boots as she dragged me back there Sunday morning. (I wasn't – that's just not my style.)

As she shopped, I observed the girl behind the counter. Customers walked in – she said nothing. Customers walked out – she said nothing. She stood there staring at her mobile device.

I was mesmerized by this display of indifference.

Customers came and went and she didn't say a word. She barely looked up.

Why does this intrigue me so much? I can think of two reasons.

First, the beginning of every interaction is the proverbial moment of truth., whether it's a sales call, a coaching session or a retail situation similar to what I've described here.

Customers are bombarded with hundreds of messages every day. The external communication that we all face is out of control – and the trick is to get people to pay attention to you. There are so many choices. I knew that just on this block in downtown Nashville, there were many other shops selling boots.

What sets these places apart? I'm sure they all have the latest styles. We know location is the same. Pricing has to be pretty similar.

It's the **people** who make the difference. Are they paying attention? Are they respecting the fact that boot customers have choices and they've chosen this shop in which to spend their time and money?

Do your people care that the customers who call or walk through the front door have given other stores the *boot*? (I'm sorry, I couldn't help myself.)

Anyway, it's the second reason that gets the wheels in my mind turning.

How do we get this individual to care?

I imagine keeping her job is an important motivator, but it goes deeper. If I were her manager, I would share how important these basic conversational skills are for her future. The greatest gift that managers give employees like her is the chance to build the skills necessary for life, like greeting people sincerely and saying thank you. Being able to start and continue conversations. Being able to ask questions and listen to the answers with mindfulness and sincerity. Complimenting others. Thinking of others.

A mistake that smart managers <u>don't</u> make is wasting an opportunity to influence young people.

Her manager could help her understand the importance of thinking about someone beside herself. This is a task made difficult by sites such as Facebook and Twitter, which practically beg users to share every intimate detail of their private lives out loud. It seems like people are forced to shout louder and louder about where they're going, what they're doing and why they're doing it. As I write this, a "friend" of mine on Facebook has posted about going to the grocery store, an animal hospital, a bookstore, the pharmacy and numerous casual dining establishments – all within the last 24 hours. Talk about one-sided, self-centered commentaries (not to mention bad food choices).

Try sharing the big picture with your people. *Instead of tying good people skills to a better company, tie them to a better person.* Tie success in selling boots in a small store in downtown Nashville to overall success in the future. Tie successful interactions with customers to success interacting in all walks of life.

Stores like our boot emporium miss such an opportunity, not only to set their businesses apart, but also to develop good young people at the same time. It's a shame, and I'm sad to say that such indifference helps customers take their story walkin' somewhere else to get their boots.

That's just the way it works!

MISTAKE 49

WEARING YOUR MASK AFTER HALLOWEEN

Halloween's over, you can take your mask off!

Remember that one? As children we'd say that to friends to give them a little grief.

Recently, I read a book called the Inspiration Factor. In this book, the author, Terry Barber, talks a bit about authenticity and the need to take off your mask (to reveal your true nature) if you want to inspire other people.

His words reminded me of a team leader I met last year. As I worked with Henry and his five sales professionals, I sensed that there was a working disconnect between him and his team. Henry didn't seem authentic to his team and thus, he had a tough time motivating them to consider what they could do to build more business and place more brands.

The reason they were disconnecting soon became clear.

See – Henry's boss, the Sr. VP of Sales, was a huge football fan. He even took a few snaps at the college level. His way of motivating was to quote Vince Lombardi and Don Shula at every opportunity. He was more a yeller and much less a listener. But Henry wasn't like that, nor did he want to be. He was more cerebral. He liked to listen more than talk and he never yelled at anybody. Still, he felt the need to put on a mask and motivate using football clichés, and that made him feel uncomfortable.

Perhaps you've heard Abraham Lincoln's legendary expression – "You can fool all the people some of the time, and some of the people all the time, but you cannot fool all the people all the time."

His team wasn't fooled any of the time. They realized they weren't getting the real deal from Henry.

Can you imagine how exhausting it must have been for Henry? Being alert at all times. Looking for the right people to impress. Saying the right words. The right quotes. It seemed that in Henry's organization, wearing the mask was more important that being authentic.

Think about your environment. Do you know anybody who wears a mask? What image does that person project? What are some ways that wearing a mask cuts down on his or her authenticity? Can you pinpoint a time that you wore a mask? How did it affect the way you interacted with others?

As I coached Henry, I suggested that there could be no trust without that authenticity (taking off the mask), and without trust, all efforts to inspire and motivate would be a waste. He had to let his people in a little to inspire them. They had to see the real Henry.

Henry's reaction was predictable. "Do I have to share all my baggage with the team?"

Please, no! Be discerning on how much to share and when to share it. Take baby steps.

I checked in with Henry last week. He remarked that as he shared more, his team began to share as well. He learned that one of the greatest motivators of all was listening. He'd ask questions, listen to the answers, share a little and listen even more. In a matter of weeks, the walls and uneasiness began to fade. As Henry shared his strengths and flaws, the team began to do the same. The coaching sessions were more intuitive and interactive and less fake. As he used fewer clichés, his people tuned in more and gave him fewer clichéd excuses in return. His coaching improved by leaps and bounds.

His team left it all on the field. (Just kidding – that's what Henry's boss used to say!)

If you're still wearing your mask - take it off. Be more real and performance will improve.

That's just the way it works. (After all, Halloween's over…)

MISTAKE 50

"WINGING SALES CALLS"

No matter where I go, sales professionals and their managers always ask me for my "#1 sales secret"; like there's some kind of magic formula for great sales and amazing execution.

Unfortunately, I have no such secrets. I wish I did!

But I do know that better preparation is as close to a secret as I can find and I believe that sales professionals are woefully underprepared for sales calls. It's the one area that falls quickly and easily to the curse of complacency.

Many professionals think that "winging it" is the way to go. It's not. Maybe it used to be, but not anymore.

Consider the following questions while preparing or helping your people prepare for their next sales call.

Are you reviewing/practicing/articulating call's objectives?

You'd be amazed at how many sales professionals enter an account with no real idea of what they intend to say or do while in the account. I believe that actually saying the objective out loud goes a long way towards your success. It builds confidence.

Is your sales professional practicing the objective statement? As I mentioned, have your sales professional practice his or her segue out loud to build conviction. A segue is a smooth transition from one topic or section to the next. In this case, I'm referring to the transition from rapport to selling, a part of the call that causes apprehension for many sales professionals. I find that if your professional spends time practicing the transition out loud, just that simple repetition will help him or her execute more effectively. If your customer sees (and feels) the conviction in your sales professional's heart, he or she may be more likely to support your products. If not, it will likely be a tough sale.

Are you reviewing relevant product knowledge?

I don't mean the knowledge you feel most comfortable sharing, but the knowledge your customer feels most comfortable hearing. There's a big difference there.

Are you anticipating retailer roadblocks?

Be it no space, no budget or "my consumers won't buy this"… Whatever the objection, are you spending time preparing for such sentiments? I bet you've heard them all before.

Are you re-familiarizing yourself with your retailer's needs and making sure you talk to the decision-maker?

Talk to as many people as possible in an account. I'm amazed at how many sales professionals stop by an account (by habit) when they know the decision-maker isn't there. NO! Schedule an appointment and, if the DM (decision-maker) isn't there, go back another time. Also, never forget to ask them these timeless questions: 1) What am I doing well? and 2) What can I do better? Ask both questions of the decision-maker (and others) at least once a quarter.

Are you revisiting past calls and re-strategizing issues?

Have you handled any open items? One way to build customer confidence is not only to do what you said, but also to mention that success at the outset of a sales call. Not boasting, just reminding. And trust me, if you didn't handle a $4 credit or similar insignificant issues, don't bother with sharing the benefits. Your customer will be thinking about anything other than what you are selling.

Are you planning to do a proper survey?

Check out your own products and those of the competition (more on checking out the competition later). How do the displays look? Neat? Disheveled? Orderly? Are the products fresh and rotated properly? Have you been maintaining your displays? Can your customer tell? Is the price clear? If not, the customer will move right past the product without even thinking twice.

Is the font big enough? Does the signage stick out? Signage should grab attention, be short, punchy, clear and easy to read while moving (if the goal is for someone to stop and buy something). Is the display accessible for consumers? In other words, can the height-challenged reach everything? According to retail expert Paco Underhill, author of many books on consumer shopping habits, the average consumer is 5 feet, 5 inches. Can shorter people reach your most profitable items?

More questions: are all prices facing out? Are the labels facing out? Is the display full? Is everything pulled forward? Did you clean out the back room? Is the display stable? Do you know the sales and velocity numbers for the display?

I know, it's a lot of questions! Try to have a few answers and make sure to identify opportunities within the account before sitting down with the decision-maker.

Are you bringing the proper sales tools?

Is your route book up to date? I know many managers who specify that route books should be updated every 90 days or so. No. How about every week? Your sales tools are crucial to your sales success.

Are you reviewing what's happening with the competition?

It's best to notice, think and act. As you survey the account, think about what you see. What competitor items have been brought in since the last visit? Are there new displays? It's one thing to notice what the competition does; it's another to react in a constructive way. Interpreting the competition's actions is the key.

Are you wiping the slate clean?

Leave any emotional baggage from prior calls in the car. Sometimes the most difficult task is entering an account knowing that the last time didn't go so well.

So what do you do when the last call wasn't so smooth?

Try for some improvement on this call. It's not about being great – it's about improving. Take action! Doing something (anything) will lead to more motivation; more success. Small acts go a long way!

So there you have it, 9 questions to help you be more prepared for the next sales call. Do you or your people have a long way to go in this area? Not to worry! Start by answering one of the many questions above and, every couple of weeks add another facet to your repertoire of skills. Spend time each morning planning out your day in the ultimate act of preparation. Even five or ten minutes will help. At the end of the day, spend another five minutes reviewing what happened.

Answer the following questions: whom do I have to follow up with? Did I make any promises that I have to record so I don't forget? Did I hit my objectives today? What can I do tomorrow, to be a little bit better than today?

So as I prepare to conclude this chapter, let me remind you that with more preparation, confidence will increase – and the sales and success will follow.

That's just the way it works.

WHAT IS A SMART MANAGER?

I hope that you've enjoyed Table for Three? and learned a few strategies to help you avoid the dumb mistakes that smart managers don't make!

As I was putting the final touches on the manuscript, it occurred to me that I hadn't defined what I consider to be a smart manager.

So, what does it take to be a smart manager?

How's this for a short answer: If you avoid a majority of the 50 mistakes described within these pages, you'll be considered a smart manager.

Can you avoid all the mistakes? Probably not, but if you avoid enough mistakes, it will make a difference.

As a result of your interactions, your associates will be *better than before.*

- Better able to sell - than before.
- More confident - than before.
- More appreciated - than before.
- Clearer on how to carry out your instructions - than before.
- More capable of solving problems - than before.
- Better at execution - than before.

Simply put, your people will be better in many, many ways than before, just because you've spent quality time with them.

So, without further adieu, lets get to the traits of a smart manager!

- A smart manager doesn't live in a vacuum. He understands that his actions affect others. He's not a weenie.
- A smart manager stresses the importance of merchandising.
- A smart manager shares how his company's products help customers.
- A smart manager doesn't automatically assume that his people are listening.
- A smart manager doesn't avoid sensitive conversations.
- A smart manager shares her feedback, more frequently than just at the yearly performance review.

- A smart manager uses more than just social media to build lasting relationships. He understands how to build rapport.
- A smart manager communicates clearly and leaves nothing to chance.
- A smart manager is candid, no matter how hard it may be for others to hear the truth.
- A smart manager creates problem-solvers, instead of just solving problems.
- A smart manager encourages one and all to contribute their ideas.
- A smart manager uses meetings for more than just dumping data on everyone.
- A smart manager doesn't allow his friends to "run the roost."
- A smart manager sets goals, and then helps her team achieve the goals.
- A smart manager asks, "How can I support you?"
- A smart manager focuses his team's energy on what's important.
- A smart manager says, "I'm sorry."
- A smart manager never gives up on a customer.
- A smart manager doesn't handle routine problems for her people.
- A smart manager listens to his people.
- A smart manager helps her team understand the basics of business.
- A smart manager controls time, instead of being controlled by time.
- A smart manager looks in the mirror and asks, "How can I improve?"
- A smart manager shows emotion, but doesn't gratuitously yell at his people.
- A smart manager learns how to effectively *coach* her people.
- A smart manager pays attention to the all his people, not just the ones who need help.
- A smart manager has the guts to help people find employment elsewhere.
- A smart manager stresses **P**ractice, **P**erseverance, **P**reparation, **P**riority, and **P**assion.
- A smart manager understands that you change a customer's mind by giving him or her additional information to make a confident, sensible decision.
- A smart manager wants timely feedback on his coaching.
- A smart manager wouldn't dare say, "Just Go Get It Done."
- A smart manager sends a positive message at all times.
- A smart manager tries, and encourages, new selling approaches.
- A smart manager sets a positive example for his people to follow.
- A smart manager doesn't let his individual's personal opinions seep in to the workplace.
- A smart manager doesn't slight her customers.
- A smart manager looks for ways to learn more about her associates and customers.

- A smart manager uses his time wisely.
- A smart manager encourages dreams, instead of squashing dreams.
- A smart manager is continually trying to learn where he stands with his people.
- A smart manager never takes the easy way out.
- A smart manager listens, more than he talks.
- A smart manager asks questions, instead of arbitrarily sharing his opinion.
- A smart manager understands that his customers don't all have the same level of importance.
- A smart manager doesn't let her team become complacent.
- A smart manager doesn't undermine his subordinates.
- A smart manager doesn't wait for someone else to take initiative.
- A smart manager doesn't waste opportunities to influence young people.
- A smart manager is authentic. He shares himself, so his people do the same.
- A smart manager helps her associates prepare for sales calls.

So, there you have it; 50 traits of a smart manager.

Do you have to change everything at once?

Absolutely not! Improvement is about taking small steps forward. It's about evolving just a little bit each day. Think evolution, not revolution.

Change one behavior this month, and another behavior next month. Over time, your skills will improve and the evidence of you making the dumb mistakes, that smart managers don't make, will disappear. You'll be better off and so will your people.

That's just the way it works.

ACKNOWLEDGMENTS

There are many people who have helped me bring this book to you and I want to give thanks to a few from the bottom of my heart:

Jill Rosen, my wife. Your support means a ton to me. I love you.

With your blessing, I've gotten to know so many sales and management professionals and become involved with numerous sales organizations. Without that interaction, I never would have had the chance to form my management philosophies. Thanks for continuing to be my best friend and laughing at my silly jokes. Thank goodness you smiled in my direction, instead of any other Glenbrook North senior!

Josh, Danny and Ben Rosen, my children. I hope you will continue the practice of making fun of virtually everything I do and having numerous laughs at my expense. I'm never sure if you're laughing with me or at me. I think the latter but who even knows anymore!

Whatever the case, you've turned into exceptional young men. Mom and I are so proud of you.

I love all you guys. Keep smiling and keep laughing.

And thanks to all the company leaders who have allowed me the pleasure of working with their sales and management teams. And to the hundreds of managers who have allowed me to enter their lives, if just for a few hours – thank you.

Keep fighting the good fight and whatever you do, stop bringing your smart phone to the lunch!

ABOUT THE AUTHOR

Everyone talks effective sales and management practices, but Darryl Rosen has lived them his entire career. He served as President and owner of Sam's Wines & Spirits, a family business started by his grandfather in the 1940's. Under his leadership and unwavering commitment to superior customer service and top-notch sales and management practices, Sam's grew from a small single operation to a multi-unit retailer with nearly $70 million in sales. Sam's reputation earned Darryl and his team an unrivaled national and international reputation.

Since selling Sam's in 2007, Darryl has taken his decades of experience from running a successful business and his interaction with thousands of hardworking, intelligent sales professionals and managers and currently consults and trains professionals who seek to strengthen their sales and management practices.

His unique consulting and training practice provides sales and management training, retailer and consumer focus group research and analysis and retailer education and events. Darryl's practice also conducts extensive research to measure the critical dynamic between managers and sales professionals and designs custom programs to improve working relationships and create better sales coaches.

Before joining Sam's, Darryl received a Bachelor's Degree in Accounting from Indiana University and became a certified CPA. He earned his MBA in Marketing and Organizational Behavior from Northwestern University, Kellogg Graduate School of Management in 1997.

Darryl enjoys spending time with his wife (Jill) and three boys (Josh, Danny and Ben), and is always hoping that this year will be the year for the Cubbies! It rarely ever is...

If you would like more information on Darryl Rosen's speeches, seminars and consulting services, please use the following contact information.

darryl@darrylrosen.com

For more tools including articles and videos and for additional ways that
Darryl Rosen can help your managers avoid the mistakes
that smart managers <u>don't</u> make…

Please visit www.darrylrosen.com

Or

www.tableforthreethebook.com

OTHER BOOKS
BY DARRYL ROSEN

Surviving the Middle Miles
26.2 Ways to Cross the Finish Line with Your Customers

Succeeding with your customers and associates requires great discipline. In his first book, Darryl Rosen will help you "survive the middle miles!" The inevitable part of any business endeavor where the excitement of the start has faded and you can't yet imagine the taste of the finish line.

Unleashing Your Inner Sales Coach
How to Inspire, Motivate and "Coach" Your Sales Teams to Success

In Unleashing your Inner sales coach, Darryl Rosen addresses the role of the middle manager (and up) and how these individuals can strengthen their team's sales and management practices. By reading this book, and adding to your skill set, you will improve your interactions, both with your sales professionals and your customers.

Winning the Customer Loyalty Marathon
How to Achieve Sales and Service Excellence in the Beverage Business

Succeeding with your customers and associates requires great discipline. In this book, Darryl Rosen will help you "win the customer loyalty marathon" and survive the middle miles. The inevitable part of any business endeavor where the hard work of kindling customer interest and keeping loyal customers is gained through building, cultivating and maintaining strong, win-win customer relationships